CHOOSE YOUR OWN

CHOOSE YOUR OWN

AN ORIENTATION MANUAL TO THE UNIVERSE

CHAUNCEY MCGLATHERY
THE HERO'S JOURNEY | VOLUME TWO

Copyright © 2022 by Chauncey McGlathery

All rights reserved. This book or any portion thereof may not be reproduced or used in any manner whatsoever without the express written permission of the publisher except for the use of brief quotations in a book review.

LIMITS OF LIABILITY AND DISCLAIMER OF WARRANTY

The author and publisher shall not be liable for your misuse of this material. This book is strictly for informational purposes. The purpose of this book is to educate and entertain. The author and publisher do not guarantee anyone following these techniques, suggestions, tips, ideas, or strategies will become successful. The author and publisher shall have neither liability nor responsibility to anyone with respect to any loss or damage caused, or alleged to be caused, directly or indirectly by the information contained in this book. Views expressed in this publication do not necessarily reflect the views of the publisher.

Cover Design: by Triv ilovedesignsbytriv@gmail.com

Printed in the United States of America
Keen Vision Publishing, LLC
www.publishwithKVP.com
ISBN: 978-1-955316-56-9

To those who are brave enough to build a life they don't need a vacation from.

TABLE OF CONTENTS

INTENTION	9
INTRODUCTION	11
Chapter One: **DISCOVERING**	27
Chapter Two: **SURVIVING**	49
Chapter Three: **MASTERING**	73
Chapter Four: **BELONGING**	91
Chapter Five: **PLAYING**	109
MEET THE AUTHOR	127
STAY CONNECTED	129

INTENTION

Forget your constraints, limitations, and obstacles. Let us sing in unison that we belong here on earth for such a time as this. Gather every failure and doubt that surfaces as we explore the universe of choices before us. Although times may be tough and challenging, we are flying through space on this spinning rock at the best time there has ever been for our gifts and possibilities.

Honor the fears, insecurities, and worries that come into focus as we embark on this journey. Bring to the forefront of the mind those things that are frightening, intimidating, and frustrating. Prepare to confront every doubt that arises as we embrace this new adventure.

The days of running away are over. The season of procrastination has passed. The time has come to build, grow, and show up. We are in this space together. At this moment, with all we have and all we have been through, we resolve to build an invincible army of hope. We will represent our authentic selves while giving honor to all who have come before us.

Raise your expectations of what can happen when we embrace our conflicts. Step away from the shadows and come out of the darkness. Connect with those who see the treacherous now as an unprecedented opportunity to reveal what the ancestors have always known.

Although insecurities have met you at every point of trial, know that the power of light within you is greater than every giant that threatens you. Before our very eyes, you can transform into your truest self with your brightest plans and intentions illuminating your consciousness. Let the neglected soul within you finally have its moment on the stage.

I pray that happiness arrives at your doorstep. May it knock early, stay late, and leave behind gifts of peace, love, joy, and good health.

Author Unknown

INTRODUCTION

Every next level of your life will demand a different you.

Leonardo Dicaprio

THE INTERVIEW

Podcast Interview Excerpt from 1/19/22

INTERVIEWER: So, how's the new book going?

ME: [It is] funny you should ask. Writing the second book has been much different than the first. My intention for the second book is much more specific. I am attempting to write a guide to the universe.

INTERVIEWER: How is that? Or, maybe I should say, what do you mean [by] a guide?

ME: Well, the first book is really about becoming comfortable in the skin you're in or merely managing your status quo. Getting to the place where you accept all that has happened as a necessary path to bring you to the here and now.

INTERVIEWER: Yeah, I read the first book, and I have to say I saw so much of myself in your text.

ME: Exactly. That's the power of the personal story. It connects us to each other. However, when we fail to embrace our story, we send mixed messages to the universe. People either struggle to comprehend or respond in a way we don't understand. But the revolutionary notion of the book is found when we discover the power we have.

INTERVIEWER: So, how is the second book different?

ME: Well, the second book picks up where the first one left off. It starts at the point of acceptance and moves into the experience of life. It's designed to share strategies and best practices for navigating the world with a renewed interest in developing the highest version of yourself that's possible. And then to reconsider and renegotiate our stories and find new ones to embrace new experiences while making sense of all the feedback you get along the way.

INTERVIEWER: Hence, a guide to the universe?

ME: Exactly. Now, I should also mention that one of the things I struggled with is raising the readers' expectations at the onset so that they get out of the mind of [a] memoir [and] into the mind of engaging with the text as a guide for themselves.

INTERVIEWER: Say more about that. What makes you feel that you have a responsibility to affect someone else's expectations of your book?

ME: Well, it's not like I want to change what others experience. I just want to make sure the person who picks up this book gets the most out of it. Oftentimes, if you think you are simply reading a memoir, you may limit its application to your life and experience. You may focus your expectation on gaining a better understanding of how that person [the author] came

INTRODUCTION

to become themselves. On the other hand, if someone says, "These stories are shared so that you as the reader might glean your own guide to interacting with and understanding the universe," then you know [to] expect to explore each story for lessons as examples, strategies, and principles that are transferable to your own life.

MY PURSUIT OF HAPPINESS

When was the last time you were happy?

If someone would have asked me that a few years ago, I would have answered that the last time I was truly happy was during my last performance or immediately afterward. You might think that someone like me, who makes his living helping others define and realize their happiness, would have found the key to this age-old question early on. But that's not my testimony.

During my youth, I was so concerned with being polite that I dared not disrupt the apple cart. Instead, I spent my time allowing others to determine the extent of my happiness. Tragically, instead of living my own life, I lived *their* lives. I competed with their imagined outcomes like gifted kids often do for their overbearing parents. Although my parents weren't that overbearing, I fell into the trap of busyness so common to fellow members of Generation X. But, something funny happened to me on the way to the grave.

I woke up.

At the point in my life when things should have been perfect for me, they weren't. Although a high-pitched whistling alarm went off deep inside me many years ago, I didn't heed it. In fact, I couldn't even hear it. I was too distracted by living the idyllic life. Then, one day, my health fell like a light fixture from the sky, and my storied life crashed.

I found myself on my back, hours away from losing my mortality. That's when the deafening silence around me got my attention. It had been there all the time. All within me had been frantically screaming as I barreled toward the cliff like Thelma and Louise. I was just too distracted to hear it.

Barricade after barricade, and I blew through them all. These internal warnings were too inconvenient for my consideration. I was hurting, grieving, and about to crash, but I did not want anyone to know. I allowed my pace to calm me down whenever my anxieties flared. Then I would go back to my routine as if nothing was wrong. I left no space in my day to stop and ask for help. I did what my dad always did and kept myself busy, hoping that I would eventually outrun my pain.

Finally, one August night in the hospital, I had an epiphany that would forever change my life. Although my body was shutting down, none of the tests my doctors performed were conclusive. That night, I had a dream that put it all into perspective. Having been born a dreamer, I thought I had experienced every type of dream. But this dream terrified and arrested me as none had done before.

MY DREAM IN THE HOSPITAL

All my life, I had always found someone else to blame for my failures. But in this dream, there were no scapegoats in the room. I appeared as a critical patient on my deathbed. That is when a strange doctor visited me in the Intensive Care Unit. He administered the final test I had to pass to survive.

INTRODUCTION

In the dream, the doctor instructed me to hold my right arm straight up in the air. Apparently, I had to do this to breathe. My lungs had stopped working, and my body was out of air. The power to remain a living soul was not in my lungs but my right arm. As long as I could hold my arm in midair, I could continue to breathe. If my arm ever dropped out of the air, I would gasp for the last time and finally give up the ghost.

Gravity eventually began to pull in a way I found harder and harder to resist. Ever so slowly, my arm began to fall. I was about to lose consciousness for the last time. As I lay dying, tremendous regret filled my heart. I had pursued what I thought was a good life. Now it was over because I had finally run out of gas. My body gave out despite my best-laid plans. That night, I accepted my imminent death as an inevitable outcome.

I cannot begin to describe the pain and agony that immediately came over me. I felt betrayed by all my life teachers. I knew this doctor had set me up to fail. In response to his instruction in my dream, I raised my arm in real life. But gravity soon had its way. I was doing everything I could to prop my arm by adjusting my body, but my inability to pass this test revealed the failure of my entire life.

CHOOSING TO REENGAGE

I had earned this impossible set of circumstances. I had created a lifestyle in which I was guaranteed to fail. And just as in my dream, there was no way I could pass this test. If somehow given a second chance, I would have to change my entire approach to life. Now that I was out of moves, I would have to learn to stop running and face myself. How would I engage in the conflict? The choice was mine to make.

The next morning, the strangest thing happened. Haunted by my virtual death, I woke up with such a start I shook the bed. My face and hospital gown were wet with tears. I had cried myself to sleep for what I thought would be the last time. In my dream, I had fought as hard as I knew how, but my body didn't have the strength to win. When I awoke on this other side of eternity, I knew I had been given a second chance.

So, I chose to engage.

The stories I had held since childhood had not emphasized any lifestyle warnings. There was no place in my life-guiding paradigm to consider disruption. I knew the work of healing would be a life-long process, but I would start line-by-line. I would reevaluate the stories I had been told and the ones I told myself. I would learn to live all over again as a baby reborn into the universe. This book is a guide to those lessons.

REORGANIZING MY LIFE AROUND SELF-CARE

Equipped with a new paradigm and a new lease on life, I vowed to reorganize my life with new priorities and values. I would rebuild my life with better parameters. I would start each day by focusing all my energy and attention on my well-being. Self-care would be my cornerstone, and my work would flow from this core of my being into the universe. I would accept my life as an example of the classic hero's journey, where all our stories weave together to support our common objective: To live the best possible life we can live. That is the goal of Volume Two of this daunting work.

INTRODUCTION

Now, I am on the other side of my life-affirming revelation. I resolve to face my insufficiencies. I will love the God in myself and the God in you as the divine light of consciousness that manifests itself as this universe. I will celebrate this divine force that makes all experiences possible, including the writing and reading of this text. I will be careful to honor the light that shines forth in wisdom as we all experience the full reality of bliss in our illuminated nature.

The number of stages in this ancient human journey depends on who you ask. I have decided to explore this quest in five separate volumes. From reading the Amazon reviews, I am excited to hear how readers have engaged so far. Whereas Volume One was about an immediate transformation of self, this second volume describes what happens when the hero pursues a quest or calling in the universe.

I have divided this second volume into five chapters. Each chapter represents a unique phase in this universal process. These chapters are in developmental order as I refer to my experiences in this journey. Each of these chapters explores a survey of my experiences and gives readers tips on how they might optimize each phase.

In the hopes that you come out better, after having contemplated these concepts, I look forward to sharing your experiences on all social media platforms. Before we launch into the deep, here are a few concepts I would like you to consider from myths and stories about heroes. I hope these help guide you as you consider your experience as the hero of your own story.

REVISITING THE STORY OF THE VINEYARD

As I meditated on the story of this book, I realized that among the important themes we are collectively experiencing in this pandemic age is this concept of fairness as balanced against the freedom to choose.

What is so interesting about landing on this thesis right now? I'll address this question in terms of two stories from my childhood.

The first related story is about workers in a vineyard. In this story, laborers arrive for work at two different times of the day. The ones who arrive just before the day is over receive the same pay as those who started early that morning. Because the second group receives the same pay, the first group thinks the system is unfair.

When I first heard this story, I did not understand the issue. Obviously, the owner should have determined the wage per hour and applied it universally. Then, regardless of when workers arrived, all would be paid according to the hours worked.

This story perfectly describes my dilemma in the hospital. I felt like the early workers, complaining about my health as unfair pay. "Wait a minute now," I said. "I'm not one of those people who ignored "righteous" principles since my youth." I knew those people, and I was proud that I was not like them. I felt deprived of even a modicum of life's happiness. In my life, I had missed the fun. Now that I was dying in my youth, nothing was fair about this trade.

What will people say when they find out what has happened to me? Won't this appear to be unfair? I think I have earned

INTRODUCTION

a better end than this. And I think they will too!

There are many nuanced lessons available in my childhood stories. However, my interests in them are derived from a context that presented the issues in Black and white contexts. I have used these stories to teach me how to make moral decisions. I should expect success with my attempts at righteousness. Because I had not reexamined these stories through a more mature lens, I only extracted the lessons that applied to kids. The lessons I needed for adulthood carefully eluded my grasp.

REVISITING THE STORY OF THE SWALLOWED MAN

The second related story is about a man who was swallowed whole. Even though this story is ancient, its mythic theme is universal. At the beginning of the story, a man is safe aboard a ship. Then, a fierce storm rises in the ocean. Superstitiously attributing the storm to his own life choices, the man volunteers to be thrown into the sea. His body falls into the dark waters like many of our ancestors in the transatlantic slave trade. He expects his body to join the legions of kings and queens on the ocean floor.

Before the storm, he had refused to save his enemy from destruction. Thus, he was thrown into the darkness with no recovery in sight. Suddenly, his fall to the earth is disrupted by a force of nature. The man in the story is swallowed whole by a whale.

As a kid, this story seemed to have very limited application. How would these circumstances ever apply to anyone else? How often does a man get swallowed by a fish? But, now that

I read it in the face of my reflective work as a hero, I realize there was much more here than I ever knew.

This man's quest reveals important lessons for me as a potential hero. The whale embodies the life or energy that is so dangerous that it must be consciously controlled. Universally, the whale shows the dangers in the ocean. The dark and stormy ocean personifies physical and tangible threats to the distracted man floating atop the water.

In addition, this ocean personifies everything dark and unknown *within* the hero. Even when the hero moves according to established norms, there always exists the danger that he will find himself in chaos, where what once was predictable now seems filled with treacherous possibilities.

The doomed man finds himself in peril because he is unwilling to challenge the lessons from the stories of his past. He refuses to upgrade his psychological operating system to save a rival culture from impending doom. In the process, he creates danger for himself. But should I blame him for running away from "his assignment?" Why should he risk his life to save his enemy? Don't enemies deserve condemnation as payment for their "evil" ways?

NEW LESSONS FROM THE SWALLOWED MAN

Peering at this story through the lens of my new life, the swallowed man of my childhood looks just like me. I could have avoided my life-threatening circumstances had I been able to glean these lessons. Finally, I can win the day and become the hero I am destined to be when I choose to extend grace, even to those I hate the most. In the process of saving my enemy, I save myself.

INTRODUCTION

As it turns out, this story is not about the adversary at all. Rather, it teaches me how to develop the hero within. I learned from this story how the energy within me can overtake my best intentions, just as my distractions overcame me. Now, I see why I must learn how to control my unconscious power and pay attention to my choice. When given the option, I must consciously choose to save even my enemies as they threaten to harm me.

I always had the choice to stop my pace and figure out what was wrong with me. But because I was determined not to grieve, I almost lost my life. My dad had just died, and I was not ready to live without him. I should have stopped to accept my grief and mourn my loss. But it was so much easier to resist the clarion call to save myself. I did not want to slow my pace and deal with my father's death. So instead, like the man in the story, I ran until I could run no more.

I never bothered to account for what life without him would be. I should have stayed and faced my fear of life without Dad. Instead of interrupting the pace of my life and seeing a therapist, I kept moving as that was the easiest thing to do.

I was afraid to accept my loss and face myself. So I abandoned my culture of honesty and tradition of authenticity and raced in the wrong direction. Beyond the threshold of strength, my psychological storm inevitably worsened. The medical crew in the hospital threw me overboard by failing to diagnose my condition. As my doctor advised me to get my affairs in order, he was certain that the monster in the darkness would finally consume me.

CHOOSE YOUR OWN ADVENTURE

CHOOSING MY ADVENTURE

How could I have missed this very basic lesson? I should have mastered this story while still in my youth. I considered myself to be far above average intelligence. So, how could this lesson about the very mechanics of the universe escape my grasp? What had I learned, if not how to come inside out of the rain?

In this story, the man is sentenced to remain for days inside his darkness. He experiences this mortal threat only because of his stubbornness. Once he realizes his mistake and accepts responsibility, he realigns himself with his destiny and emerges on the shore. He has a renewed interest in living out the fulfillment of his assignment, even if it means he has to reconstruct his identity and values from the ground up.

Now that he knows who he is, both he and his enemies can finally be saved from their imminent destruction. Ideally, he is now reborn with a new character, a new life, and a new meaning in the universe. This meaning isn't defined by others but by the standard of what he was meant to be.

By ensuring that others saw me as exceptional, I fell into greed and selfishness. I also found myself in unsustainable trouble. This reflects a conceit for where I was and what I thought I had earned. This misalignment between my mind and my soul almost cost me my life. What a shame it would be to lose eternity in a selfish pout. One of the reasons I didn't die that summer was because I pulled from the wealth of my ancestors' stories. Their words caught me like a guardrail when I drove myself off the healthy road.

Universally, this man teaches me that it is my quest to find

INTRODUCTION

my place within these stories and myths. I am created to live in accord with all of humanity. But to do so, I must commit myself daily to this task. And there are dire consequences for consistently missing this mark.

Now, I don't regret any aspect of my life. In fact, for the first time, I can truly say I love just being me. I have decided to devote all my energy to sharing my love and life. I have vowed to help my friends become better versions of themselves just for themselves. I will help others avoid the kind of pitfalls that almost killed me.

What an important time to arrive at this point.

As you consider this text, I will prepare you to respond to challenges better than I did. You can learn from my mistakes without ever risking your own life. Then, maybe you can glean even more lessons old stories provide. Each one responds to our dilemmas from the perspective of becoming a hero. If we heed them, we can avoid the pitfalls on this path.

THE OPPORTUNITY OF THIS PRESENT AGE

Right now, our community is right in the middle of both of these childhood stories. People are becoming obsessed with our current cultural storms. Meanwhile, we are missing the point of what we have and what we can do. Instead of cooperating, we are distracted and rudely complain. We have forgotten the grace that comes with being alive.

As the so-called inventors of the modern ideal of freedom, we feel as if we can define what it means to be free. Looking close, we may find ourselves among the villains in our community. Like the early workers, we think we know so much better than everybody else. I almost lost my life worrying about what everybody else thought about me. That's exactly why I had to write this book.

As independent humans on this planet, we get to decide the kind of lives we want to live. That is the way the universe is designed. But regardless of the choices we make, there will be consequences. Trying to live for others almost cost me my life. But luckily, I was given another chance. *And I am going to take it!*

THE OPPORTUNITY FOR THE READER

I have cracked a code that will help you navigate the universe. Incidentally, this volume builds off the lessons of the first. Whereas the first book helps you love and accept yourself for who you are, this second volume explains how to navigate yourself in life's challenges among the masses.

I have become a more authentic version of myself than before. I would like to pass this wisdom on to you. You should know that reading about my work does not take the place of doing your own, but I would like to offer help by giving you cliff notes of my process. I will give you the whole truth as best as I understand it. It will be uncomfortable for me and, perhaps, even for you. But in the end, it will be worth the energy we use in the process.

If you dare to dream, I will show you that there are ports of wisdom beyond our current lives. There are spaces in our collective wisdom where conflicts of truth and the false realities we desperately cling to in despair can be released and exchanged for light, goodness, and consciousness. You will learn to choose your adventure and allow others to do the same. With these tools, you can do what I have done and put your life back together again.

If you reflect on your experiences as I relay mine in this text, you will come out on the other side in a much better position than wherever you are now. You will be able to put all of your energy into who you are in the universe and not let anyone else's activity affect you. You will be able to focus only on being a better you than ever before. You will fight the temptation to compare who you are or what you have with anyone else. You will transcend whatever disruption or chaos that has come into your life.

We will emerge on the other side of these conflicts, having learned our lessons. We will be prepared for the adventures of living in the universe yet to be revealed. Join me in these next few chapters as I share five lessons of adventure that I have chosen to live by as a part of the second phase of my hero's journey.

In the following five chapters, I will highlight, as best I understand them, all of the ridiculous obstacles placed in the path of those of us who desire to live more authentic lives. I will help you experience the realization that, like me, you are not separate from consciousness itself. Working with you will be my path and work.

These five chapters represent the five aspects of this second phase in the hero's journey. They are Discovering, Surviving, Belonging, Mastering, and Playing. Although these chapters are presented in order of progression, these stages are not mutually exclusive. Depending on the issue, you could survive in one aspect while struggling to master another. And that is okay. Every hero's process is different. And believe it or not, you are a hero. Trust me. If I am, you are too.

As you dive into this ocean of experiences, may you be inspired with an everlasting joy that knows no limitation until you become perfectly aware of your greatest possibilities. I hope I one day find you dancing under waterfalls of your own forgiveness for not coming to this awareness earlier during any of the missed opportunities you had in the past.

I have a dream that the new 21st-century militancy which has engulfed our community must not lead us to lose faith in the God-nature of people, for many of our would-be enemies, as prophesied by great leaders, teachers, and prophets of the 20th Century, will be present here in the great awakening happening all over our universe. I believe that through great trial and tribulation, they will come to realize that their destiny is tied up with ours, and their liberation is inextricably and eternally linked to the liberation of all historically oppressed people.

Rev. Dr. Martin Luther King, Jr.

We are here at this moment with every possibility and potential yet before us, and we will choose together; regardless of the chaos, regardless of the odds that are stacked against us, we represent ourselves, and all of our stories and all of the dreams that place in us a position of power to have the greatest chance of our mortal existence to become the power that we are called to be. Now allow your hands to find a resting place at your sides as we begin to breathe into the reality that is greater than anything we've known.

Chauncey McGlathery

CHAPTER ONE
DISCOVERING

You will either step forward into growth or you will step back into safety.

Abraham Maslow

If the path before you is clear, you're probably on someone else's.

Carl Jung

I always wanted to be a hero. Since I was a nappy-headed little boy, those were always my favorite stories. Before beginning my current practice of self-reflection, I would have said that the hero rises above the normal human experience. And for the majority of my life, that was my driving motivation.

I got out of bed every day to make my dad proud of me. I wanted to turn my ordinary limited self into the stuff of legends. I wanted to be a leader in American life and society. So I did everything I could to distinguish myself from my peers.

Whether it was designed to garner public accolades or open esteem from my father, I was all in. I was desperate to prove that I was indeed worthy of the good fortune into which I was born. And, for decades, I worked tirelessly to make good of my life. If someone said my name, I wanted everyone to affirm this legacy; with resounding certainty, they would be eager to testify on my behalf that I graciously lived for something bigger than my self-interests. I did not even see the irony because I never spoke these words aloud.

But if I was going to be a hero, the first thing I needed to do was lose the glasses. I always hated these wheelchairs for the eyes. My dad and brother did not wear them, but somehow, I needed them. *What was wrong with me? Why wasn't I born with perfect sight?* That should have been the first clue that something would be different about my life, but I tried with all my might to ignore the hint.

In fact, bad eyesight was the second impairment I had. I was born incredibly pigeon-toed. Remember those braces Forrest Gump wore at the beginning of the movie? Those were mine. Somehow, I refused to let them cramp my style. But wearing those things for the first three years of my life had to affect me. I came into the world needing a special dispensation of technology. No one else in my family of manly men seemed challenged from the gate.

Take the hint, Chauncey. Your life is going to be different.

But they say when you have one impairment, another skill develops to help you compensate. So, I was on the lookout for some superpower to balance all my challenges. Would I develop x-ray vision and the ability to fly? Like many kids, I spent my happiest times with a pillowcase tucked inside the back of my shirt. I pretended to be Superman. But Superman does not wear glasses.

DISCOVERING

MY CHILDHOOD AS A HERO-IN-TRAINING

Perhaps that is also why I loved my riding toys so much. I used my childhood play to rehearse heroism. At four, I started with a Big Wheel. Remember those? They were yellow and black with wheels larger than life. I would dart out of my driveway, with my dad standing near the mailbox. He watched on both sides of the hill to ensure no cars were coming. Then, when I heard him yell, *"Go!"* I would pedal as if my life depended on it. Across our street, Doak Drive, I sped onto Joppa Circle, one of the neighborhood's most notorious playgrounds.

At six, I grew out of the Big Wheel and into the Huffy Green Machine, which had more power and actual gears to shift. By this time, I was able to negotiate the traffic alone under the supervision of my dad, who would watch from the front yard until I crossed. This time, I waited for my voice to permit me to cross the street, carrying my vehicle. Then, once on Joppa Circle, I would call myself to ready my engine and *Go!*

Once I turned eight, my bike lost its training wheels, and I could pedal to my heart's content on Lockie, another street that bordered our lot. I met my first girlfriend there but would not kiss her until a few years later. Then came the "big boys" bike — my ten-speed. I found it at Service Merchandise, and it looked like a luxury vehicle to me. It was tan with brown handlebars, and the remote radios had just come out. So, with my dad's help, I mounted my portal to the culture on the handlebars, which picked up the local AM signals and the FM stations.

I would tag along with Frederick, my best friend next door to my house. We rode bikes all over the entire neighborhood. I met most of the friends I have now on those bike excursions. As kids, we had no care in the world. Nothing was better than free days of exploring northwest Huntsville.

MY CALLING TO BE A HERO

Sometimes, though, I liked to ride alone. I would imagine myself as a detective, taking care to watch all those who needed my protection. I would take a pen and a little notepad in my pocket. Whenever I saw a car I did not recognize, I would write down the license plate number and wait for crime to ensue. Eventually, I would collect about ten license plate numbers and end my adventure for the day. Then, I would head back home with WEUP-radio playing "Fantasy" by Earth, Wind & Fire.

Today, Huntsville's radio waves, like everyone else's, are creatively challenged. Even in a town this size, corporations tell us what we should like. But back then, our local DJs played the best Black music. If you had the patience, you would hear all the latest records.

You could wait several hours for your song to come on. Then, as long as the DJ did not talk too far into the song's introduction, you could record your copy of the latest jam on a cassette and play it repeatedly at your convenience. My childhood playtime was the birth moment of the mixtape and one of the greatest pleasures of my young life.

Although I could not travel beyond the square of our lot unless I was in the car with my parents, I could travel in my mind with the music. Cameo, Sister Sledge, Parliament-Funkadelic, Stevie Wonder, and The Bar-Kays exposed me to new ideas and possibilities. I accessed this world inside my head. I explored Planet Rock without a chaperone and lived fully in those worlds, tethered only by my need to clean my room.

MY DAD: THE HERO

Being a Black kid in Alabama was not as challenging as all that. Most of the stories I heard about Alabama were negative or limiting, but I lived in the house with a pioneer. My dad had challenged Governor George Wallace and the demons of Jim Crow. I was my dad's son, and he was celebrated within and outside of our community. With the help of the Kennedys, he made quite a success of the engineering life at the National Space and Aeronautics (NASA) Administration at Redstone Arsenal. So, my quest to turn my impairments into superpowers was within the realm of my possibility.

One of my earliest options for achieving hero status was through my schoolwork. Even as a kid, I was aware of my dad's reputation for excellence. My academic pursuits would pick me up where Earth, Wind & Fire left off.

I remember being critical of our curriculum, even at an early age. There was not much rigor in kindergarten. We did not do any of the things my brother's class did. I already knew my numbers and letters. My favorite activity was racing to write the numbers 1 to 100 in those little boxes. I always finished about ten minutes before the rest of the class. I had started learning numbers years prior. *My dad would not have been impressed if he had been in the classroom to witness my speed.*

At recess, we could go out into the yard to play. Although I did not need a break, I enjoyed the time with my friends. We played everything – Red Light - Green Light, Tag, and Freeze Tag. These were the original "Squid Games."

Eventually, I would pull away and do my own thing. I would find a caterpillar doing his own thing, too, and we would connect. I am still fascinated by the life cycle of a caterpillar, its cocoon's design, and the butterfly's wingspan. This must be the coolest transformation in the universe. I remember trying to bring one back into the classroom, but stealth was not my ministry.

On my first day of school, I ran from the elementary school parking lot, where we dropped off my brother. *I told you to wait on me. What the hell are you running for!* My dad almost whipped me, but soon he would know why I deserved a break. After all, my legacy began that day. I was on my way to becoming a hero, just like him.

MY GRANDMOTHER: THE HERO

After school, I would be picked up by Annie Cross. Frederick's aunt would take me to the neighborhood where my dad's mother lived. That was the downtown area of Huntsville in what we called "the projects." If there was a hero in my life other than my dad, it was his mother — Mama Anna.

She lived in government-subsidized low-income housing.

Mama Anna was fierce. Everybody loved and respected her. Watching her take care of the people in that neighborhood profoundly impacted me, and I am a different man because of her.

Dad loved Mama Anna with a language that had become all too familiar. They would argue about everything, including the sun. Even though Dad was smart, Mama Anna was the wisest person I knew. Because she liked me and loved to teach, we got along really well.

Mama Anna did not take any flack from my dad. Then, he was the H-N-I-C and a big man on campus at NASA. But she could put him in his place and get him together right quick and in a hurry. To add insult to injury, she battled him with a chuckle and the widest grin on her face.

INSECURITIES OF A HERO

My dad was the most confident man in the city. His style and his strut told you everything you needed to know. He was not "new age" but very rough around the edges. In his childhood, his dad left them and started another family. So at 13, my dad became the head of his household.

It took me decades to be able to give my dad a break. I could not appreciate how his life experiences shaped his identity. I resented his diminished capacity to maintain healthy relationships. Certainly, he had the choice to be different and simply chose not to do the work, I thought. Turns out, it was not as easy for him as rocket science.

But if there was someone to turn my boring life into that of a hero, it was my dad. I remember wanting to get attention and affection from him all the time. I would come to the edge of the living room on the step near the TV. I would wait anxiously for him to see me standing there.

I had hard feelings about how he and my mother argued so often. As a hero, I wanted to help her communicate with him. He would just stare at the news while I waited at his side. I knew he cared about her, but her independence, maybe, not so much. When I approached him with concern, he would not connect with me. I would try to ask him something to break his train of thought. After getting a thumbs up or down, I would get lost back in my room.

My personality as a kid was much more like my mother's. Gifts and money were Dad's primary love language. We, on the other hand, preferred words and acts of affection. I never doubted that Dad loved us all. But he relied on his salary to erase all second thoughts.

I did not always understand him, but I always admired him. In fact, for most of my childhood, I was in a state of awe. He knew everything or at least convinced me that he did. And if anything ever hurt him, he never showed it. Like Superman, my dad was made of steel.

THE STRONG MAN OF THE NEIGHBORHOOD

Our street, Doak Drive, was a simple street in an average Black neighborhood in northwest Huntsville, Alabama. We had the largest lot on the block, sitting on a small hill. If memory

DISCOVERING

serves, it was an acre and a quarter. We had a basketball goal in our front yard that hosted kids who wanted to play.

Basketball goals were quite the commodity on Doak Drive, and my dad would hoop with anybody who wanted to take him on. That is how he established his reputation for coaching and mentoring all of the kids in our generation. Everybody loved my dad, and he treated all of the kids in the community like sons.

I thought of my dad as "the strong man," but not quite a bully. I never mentioned to anyone else how I felt about him, but Mama Anna had a way of knowing things that nobody told her. When she wanted to humble him in front of Ma or me, she would tell us that one of his legs was shorter than the other. "That's why he'd strut when he walked."

Before he died, my dad confided in me that he chose to play the role of the bad guy. It was his intention in the family dynamic to take all responsibility. He would make me and my siblings think that, regarding the tension between our parents, he was always at fault. He wanted us to see our mother as perfect. To do that, he covered many of her faults. He allowed us to blame him for any divisive energy in our household.

As he shared, I just watched his lips move, but I did not understand the words coming out of his mouth. Now that he has passed and there are no more distractions, the truth is clear. Even though Ma laughed when I told her what he had said, I now understand how my dad protected her. And I love him more now than I ever did before.

CONFLICTING PARADIGMS OF A STORIED HERO

Dad was not the guy you could share your feelings with. That made my childhood more difficult than normal. It was extremely awkward for me because my emotions were all over the place. But back then, there was no space for that sentiment in our house. I knew my dad cared for me because he paid the power bill and the mortgage. In our house, there was no space for hard feelings. You accepted what you saw and appreciated what you got.

Even before adolescence, I found myself caught in the middle of conflicting paradigms. On the one hand, my dad told me that I was alive for a purpose. He informed me that I was supposed to stay in school and go to college. Then I would be able to get a great job and provide for a family with kids who would repeat the cycle all over again.

On the other hand, Mama Anna told me that I was alive just like nature was alive. She said I was created just to be here and that it was okay for me to be beautiful and strange. According to her and my mother, I did not need to achieve anything to be valid in my humanity. But because I had not developed any voice to explain my quandary, I suffered in silence.

While the other guys were shooting basketball in the front yard, I was in the living room on the piano. If the windows of our house were open, you would hear my rendition of Hanon's Virtuoso Exercises all around the neighborhood. I was a favorite student of my piano teacher, Mrs. Inez Booth. I did not know it at the time, but she was the music department chair at Oakwood College, and she was acclaimed. My musical prowess was assured as long as I did everything she told me. I could have become a classical pianist if I had kept taking lessons in middle school, but I was not really into recitals. I decided I wanted to be onstage with other performers instead of just a solo act. So, I stopped taking lessons and joined the band.

MY INABILITY TO CHOOSE MY OWN IDENTITY

I did not live in a neighborhood that allowed kids to negotiate their identities. I was not yet about that pioneer life, at least not at that stage. I had everything I wanted, but my childhood was not easy. I probably would have become a fragile and brittle kid both in personality and experience if I thought I could have gotten away with it. But I was confident that my dad would not have tolerated it.

Dad was the psychological architect of our family. Growing up with my dad, nothing was ever open for debate. In the house of a scientist who believed that if there was no evidence for it, it did not exist, anything I experienced without scientific evidence was outside the paradigm.

No wonder I gravitated emotionally toward my mother and Mama Anna. They provided space for my questioning, energetic, and spiritual self. The women in my life seemed to have the capacity to sit with experiences and imaginations that did not show up in scientific experiences. They taught me how to make space for what I did not fully comprehend.

To this day, I remain grateful for the time I had to speak with these venerable women. Their way of loving and looking at the world was larger than that of the men I knew. Not only did they make space for my questions, but they also affirmed my doubts and celebrated them as evidence of something deep beneath the surface. They were excited as I experimented with possibilities and discovered what all was down there.

HEROES IN CHILDHOOD RELATIONSHIPS

During the day, I would go into her room as an inquisitive four-year-old. I followed her around the house, as was my custom, and watched her get ready for the day. My mother was not always happy back then. That is probably why I felt like she needed my emotional support.

It was easy to connect and create my own space in her world. During the night, however, my life took on a different shape. Connections could not happen while I was alone. This is where my intuition for inner work began to pay off. I learned to soothe myself.

In adulthood, with the loss of that maternal space, I lost the ability to maintain my spiritual alignment. But back then, I was a pro, and self-work was something I had been an expert in since birth. As a kid, I permitted myself to entertain phenomena that I still cannot explain today. So, whatever I experienced then that was not articulable or scientific with words with my conscious mind found its way into my consciousness through my dreams.

DISCOVERING

DREAMS TO SAVE MY HEROIC IMAGINATION

This was the turning point. My dreams gave me an experience of life that was not limited by rules. These experiences are governed not by words but by images and symbols. Laws of physics and gravity meant nothing in my dreams. All of the rules I was governed by were suddenly gone. What's more, I had the courage in my dreams to admit my disappointment in a way I never could express in real life.

The only problem in my dreams was waking up. Returning to my life after such great adventures felt so defeating. I soon grew tired of waking up in my same old boring life. And eventually, I realized that nothing would change for me until I changed it. This was when I began to imagine a more exciting existence.

I used music to project my dreams into my personality. If you had ever seen me on stage as a kid, you would know what I am talking about. Friends from school would come to see me perform and tell me later how I seemed like a different person. Even as an adult, being onstage turned my spark into a flame. I would fill the room with an energy that convinced and persuaded. The heroic life I had dreamed of having in childhood would still be possible if I could only realize my dreams.

The magic I experienced in dreams defied all explanations. If George Lucas could have seen my dreams as a kid, *Star Wars* would have been a choose-your-own-adventure film. The Skywalker storyline gave shape to my greatest imagination. That is when I learned that the reality in which we live is only limited by what we know to be possible. However, beyond our reality lies many potentialities that most of us will never consider, much less experience.

In my dreams, I could run faster than anyone. I had no frailties and no insecurities. In my dreams, I often become invisible so that I can move among my family and learn what they are whispering about behind closed doors. I could shoot a basketball perfectly from any spot in the gym. And, in football, I could fly and score touchdowns on every play.

Nothing could frustrate my will in my dreams. And the best part was that I never had to worry about making my dad happy with my performance in my dreams. I was a god in my dream life, and whatever I wanted to experience happened without delay.

I got to the point where I could decide what to dream and then dream it. And, if I did not like the way the last dream ended, I could go back to sleep the next night and change the ending. Dream life was easy, and I was excellent at everything I tried. But I could not stay asleep; I had work to do. And in my real life, my dad was the boss.

TRAINING TO BECOME AN HEROIC MAN

As a kid, I never doubted that I would survive everything that would happen in my life. I was trained to command an army of survivors. Even though Dad instructed me in all those things, that awareness and consciousness of transformative leadership were written in my DNA even before my birth. It flowed through my bloodstream. It filled my lungs and my imagination. Then, I was born into it. Having the kind of older brother I had made my destiny irrefutable. Ivan had unquenching, unflinching buy-in to my dad's plan and the ability to prepare us for battle. He modeled for me what the persona of a soldier needed to be, and given our family, our community, and our context, I never questioned it, even when I wanted to.

As a Black boy growing up in the post-Civil Rights American South, my father and older brother modeled manhood in every endeavor. Several moments in childhood would serve as rites of passage. These initiations and rituals provided the most foundational stories of my identity. Many of the things I did as a kid were specifically designed to build my values and shape my character.

I would also simultaneously learn how to hold my rightful place within our tribe and society. The rules were established according to my family and culture. I was trained from boyhood to be a guardian of my extended family and community. I was engineered to become the brand of man that my father was. So, I would be respected if I followed the rules of conduct as outlined in my process.

THE BARBERSHOP AS A RITE OF PASSAGE

I first noticed my process around the age of two or three or whenever I got my first haircut. This would become the single most consistent social feature of my childhood besides church on Sundays, of course. My dad was a pastor, and the sanctuary on Sunday was not optional.

However, the barbershop reserved for Saturday mornings was, at first, quite a chore. Here, I was made to bask in the stories of the elders. These men wore machismo on their sleeves and defended the race with every fiber of their posed existence. If there was diversity among them, I never perceived it. This was less of an orientation and more like an initiation. I got my monthly dose of manhood from the hands of the entire community.

While I was spared direct confrontation or interrogation for the first few years, very soon after I started first grade, I was interrogated about myself and my life. *How did I perform in school? What was my favorite subject? What was my girlfriend's name? Was she, in fact, cute, or was she the only girlfriend I could get?* And then, of course, *how did I want my hair cut?*

DISCOVERING NEW HEROISM IN OLD MEDIA

There was a large chart on the wall, no doubt produced by the Bronner Brothers Black hair care company in Atlanta. This chart featured boys and men wearing the latest styles of the late seventies. I recognized most of these styles from the one tv show with an all-Black cast at the time — *Soul Train*. There were only about five channels on the TV back then. So for the several hours we spent in the shop, we mostly watched sports or maybe westerns.

But eventually, the revered Don Cornelius would grace the stage of *Soul Train*. Then, I would be transported into a world with no rules or limitations. *Soul Train* was filmed in

Chicago, Illinois, a mecca of Black culture worldwide. Their styles, expressions, music, and life were the majority rule. Soul Train displayed the multiverse of possibilities in the African Diaspora. And we shared in this chocolate freedom as dreamers and consumers of this Black-utopian life.

As I locked my eyes on the screen, these possibilities were beamed directly into my consciousness. There, I became transfixed by life outside of the cradle of the Confederacy. In the middle of all of that noise and posturing, I imagined the day that I would be able to cross that Mason-Dixon line to freedom. Then I would be free of all expectations and constraints. On the other side of my repressed existence, I would define myself and become my own man. But here, in the meantime, Mr. Battle's chair had just opened. And after several patient hours, I was finally *next!*

As always in the barbershop, the elders were debating the hot topics of the day. After covering every aspect of gossip the neighbors had conjured, next up for debate was Christian philosophy or "soul-salvation." I tried to pay attention, but the stakes of this conversation would elude me for several more years. I would not have a voice in this place until high school. Until then, in meekness, I just listened and observed.

DISCOVERING NEW RITUALS OF PASSAGE

Another important space for me to revisit in this process of renegotiation was my family church. Here is another space I frequented, not by choice, but because my family required it. The messages I got about identity and destiny in the barbershop were always the same. However, the messages I got at church on Sundays were all over the place.

When I was a kid, the main messages were communicated to me in the form of stories. There was no thinking around theory or sociology, or even wellbeing. There was no hint of thoughtful analysis the human condition, just stories. These stories were designed to control your behavior or "encourage" you to make better choices to save your life.

Nobody chose to go to hell, which, according to Reverend Townsend, was where I easily deserved to be. This was so by the sheer degree of evil you could commit. Your fate was doomed, and there was nothing you could do to prevent it. It was not your fault but addressing it was your responsibility.

Under this old paradigm, you were not empowered to define your reality. The reality was defined by the community who knew better than you. If you wanted to participate, your choice was binary. Either you wanted to save yourself from eternal damnation, or you did not. Either you were good or bad.

If you choose the good path, you will give up your freedom. You surrendered your will by "giving your life to God." As we were taught to understand, God willingly accepted your sacrifice, which would be more than a reasonable gift on your part, and exceptionally gracious on "his."

And then, on that fateful day of judgment, you would get a pass, and your eternity would be guaranteed by a redeemer. You would live in heaven with your family in a place where there is no more death, crying, or suffering.

DISCOVERING

Only howdy, howdy, and never goodbye.

THE FLAWS WITHIN THE MATRIX

You suspected that there was something awry with many stories you were told in childhood. But no one ever questioned it, so maybe you never tried. And to make matters worse, not only could they get you with behavior, but you could also get in trouble for your thoughts. *Whose imagination could be as troubled as yours and still be forgiven?*

What was inferred but never stated is that this way of thinking required an acceptance of a black-and-white conception of reality. In this paradigm, we accepted that we experience the world in binary opposites. The problem with this idea is that the world itself is not binary. We know this intuitively, but concretely, we construct and reinforce this binary phenomenon in our everyday lives.

People are said to be either good or bad, as if all of the elements of character and personality can be reduced to one definitive judgment. But no one dares to tell you that you are nuanced and varied with moods and circumstances. So is everyone else. In fact, what appears light one day looks like darkness the next or one of the infinite shades of gray in between.

EXPLORING THE POSSIBILITIES

The spaces that we are forced to occupy as children are the places where our identities are formed. But because we never chose them, we think they are not important in adulthood. In renegotiating my strategy for healthy living, these spaces are critically important.

I have to revisit those spaces to renegotiate my core identity. I unpack what I accepted as truth without ever being given a choice. Where were those critical spaces during your childhood? Where were you forced to go and remain regularly? What did you learn about your family and your community there? What aspects of those lessons served you for a time but may no longer serve you?

Your ability to discover your possibilities is found in those spaces. That is why we start with the topic of Discovery. The attention you give now to those places will empower you to adapt and evolve into the version of yourself that you were created to be. Sure, this version of you will gain the notice of your family, friends, and coworkers. But what matters is that you will be healthier and happier.

To make progress in identity-work, you have to focus. Even though you were not paying attention to what you were gleaning, your memories survived. You can now return to those places and capture what was going over your head back then. Each memory can become richer than the one before. You can regain the power to become the version of you that you wished you had imagined then.

You spent multiple hours of quiet time in noisy spaces. You listened and observed what those who had gone before you had to say about their experiences. Now that these stories can be contrasted with your existence, you can show up and exist in those spaces, not as a representative of your family or culture, but as your authentic self.

DISCOVERING

This work does not happen in one sitting. Your identity did not take shape in one moment in time. Instead, this process of maturation took effect in repeated occurrences. You also understood that almost no step or experience in our maturity is ever a once-for-all event.

Likewise, effective rediscovery requires little or no distraction. With focus, you will eventually appreciate what is real and what is not. You will not only hear what is said around you and about you but also what was never said. As an evolved, empowered soul, you will have the ability to challenge others' opinions about you. You can confront those opinions whenever and wherever you like. When you can answer those questions about who you are with clear understanding, a pure and rooted intention will ground the person you want to be.

I have no right to call myself one who knows. I was one who seeks, and I still am, but I no longer seek in the stars or in books; I'm beginning to hear the teachings of my blood pulsing within me. My story isn't pleasant, it's not sweet and harmonious like the invented stories; it tastes of folly and bewilderment, of madness and dream, like the life of all people who no longer want to lie to themselves.

Hermann Hesse

As we begin to launch into this text, we celebrate survival and the spirit inside us that never quit. And we promise ourselves that as our challenges come to our minds and consciousness, we will learn from every failure and make room for new strategies to help us rise to the occasion that this terrible hour in the universe presents and we shall be better, better versions of ourselves that we ever imagined so that we will end this day with no regrets. And with it all we say together, Amen.

Chauncey McGlathery

AFFIRMATIONS

I am free to choose the way I will experience the world.

I am unencumbered by my past experiences and relationships.

I am honest with myself about my feelings.

I am taking each moment as a valuable opportunity to learn more about myself, my surroundings, and my possibilities.

I am confident that I will end this day with more courage than I started.

I am a unique member of the class of creatures fearfully and wonderfully made in the image of God.

CHAPTER TWO
SURVIVING

If you want to awaken all of humanity, then awaken all of yourself, if you want to eliminate the suffering in the world, then eliminate all that is dark and negative in yourself. Truly the greatest gift you have to give is that of your own self-transformation.

Lao Tzu

In Chapter One, I outlined my childhood of discovery. I shared the barriers I had to overcome to even imagine my potential. I shared how I used academics and tokens of success to compensate for my insecurities. Finally, I describe the contrasting influences of my upbringing and how I used rituals and rites of passage to construct my basic frames of reference.

Using my life as an example, you can follow a similar roadmap. Build for yourself time to spend in spaces without distraction. When you create this space, a natural repair will take place. You will find your options expanding instead of contracting, and your level of happiness will increase at every stage.

In this second chapter, I will discuss the developmental stage of surviving. I will describe the different ways heroes learn to survive. Even my dream life played a significant role in mapping my universe. I will conclude with the additional rites of passage that brought me into adulthood.

LOSING MY MOMENTUM

As long as I performed the rat race routine, my head was well above water. I had spent my entire childhood preparing for the days of being an adult. When my pace slowed to normal, I lost all forward momentum. I began to dread my days and lose emotional stability. I doubted myself and my plans for fulfilling my dreams. I began to lose faith that I could function without moving quickly through the earth.

On a whim, I decided to start waking up and getting dressed, even with nowhere to go. I cleaned up my room and showered regularly like I had someplace important to be. That is when my drive began to catch me in mid-step. My plans and future met me on the other side of my routine. I slowly began to evolve into my higher self again, one moment at a time.

The lessons I learned from my childhood stories helped create my public persona. But after suffering great loss and hardship, I revisited all I thought I knew. I learned to slowly forget the limitations I had learned. I replaced them with possibilities that I had not realized were always there.

Sometimes, the world can be harsh in how it teaches lessons. Once the platform of discovery is firmly established in the hero's psyche, the next hurdle to overcome is survival. Being able to take a direct hit squarely in the jaw is the second requirement on this quest.

LOW-FREQUENCY LIVING

When I focused on pleasing others, I became a version of my lower self. I dreamed of an authentic presence. I was worried that I would not be accepted. I found power and courage in external living, but I had never seen a man be truly vulnerable and accept his faults.

The internal journey from our lower to higher self requires more energy than any externally heroic one. Our main gift to the community won't be a fantastic resuce of someone else, but instead will result in a healthy version of ourselves. However, we must first acknowledge the barriers to our healthy existence. These will include but are not limited to anxieties, depression, and recovery from all traumatic exposures.

I was taught that you cannot change who you are. I believed that the renegotiation of my identity was not possible. So like my father, I left as little to chance as possible. I took matters into my own hands to secure a good future for myself and my would-be dependents. And I focused on the one thing I thought I could change — the world.

THREE DREAMS OF A STALEMATE LIFE

This survival strategy worked for so long that I thought it was invincible. But when I got sick, I hit a wall and ran out of "moves." That is when I found myself in the position of checkmate. There had to be a better way and I found it in my dreams. That is how I discovered three different types of hero journeys. From these stories, I found the paradigm I present in this volume.

In some of my childhood stories, the hero would follow an animal and be carried into a scene they had never imagined. This is a dream I have had since childhood. At a certain point, the animal would change into an unrecognizable being of unimaginable scope and size. Then, we would fight. I undertook this quest without a clear intention. But I suddenly found myself in an adventure I had never chosen.

Second is the kind of journey into which the hero is thrown. I rarely have this dream anymore. In this instance, you are selected into a kind of service, perhaps leadership in the military or a social or spiritual assembly. Although you do not intend it, you accept it as your destiny.

In my experience, one who has this dream must undergo a type of death of their old self and resurrection of the new. I only have this dream when something drastic needs to shift in my life. And every time I have it, I make a major life change.

The last time I had this dream, I quit my job as a musical director at a church and taught musicology courses in Boston College's African and African Diaspora Studies department. This was the one job I imagined as a very young child, but I was certain it would never come to pass after choosing a different degree path. Although my dad was livid at the thought, I was terribly excited at the prospect of teaching as this opportunity was off my current path. I will never forget the dream I shared with him as I was about to leave my prepared career path.

ME: *Well, in my dream, I was coming out of my apartment. Walking toward my car. Well, it wasn't my car, really, but in the dream, it was my car. And there was a plant or something coming out the back. And so I opened the trunk, and there was a large green plant like a vine with big leaves growing out of the trunk.*
DAD: *And?*
ME: *And that's it.*
DAD: *So what does that mean?*
ME: *That means that I have been focusing too much on myself. I need to have a job with greater impact on the community. So I told my supervisor that I quit.*
DAD: *You quit your job?*
ME: *Yeah.*
[He pauses for several seconds.]
DAD: *I think you need to ask for your job back.*
[Sigh.]

In the third type of dream from my childhood, I met an older guide who charged me in my dream to go and find my father, a recurring dream I still have to this day. It makes sense to me because this is a common dream recorded throughout human history and is referred to as the father quest. In this story, the subject experiences this dream when they are in search of the nature of their career or maybe the source of life. On this kind of journey, the hero pursues this goal deliberately with clear intentions.

CHOOSE YOUR OWN ADVENTURE

THE ANXIETIES OF AN EMPATH

My dad and I had similar anxieties. I worked hard to have a healthier experience of those anxieties than he had, but until recently, I was unsuccessful. My dad was also a dreamer. That is where I got it from. Dad was always more conservative than me. And he was never rash.

He would always carefully line up an alternative future before risking whatever potential he had. I am reminded of his law school offer, which he did not accept because of the kids he had at home. He applied and gained admission before considering abandoning his current career. Then, second-guessed himself until he eventually decided not to leap.

But my dad's claim to fame was leaping. That is what I admired most about him. It established him as a leader in our community. Even Governor George Wallace had not stopped him. With the help of the Kennedys and the national guard, my dad made history in 1963 as the first Black student admitted to the University of Alabama in Huntsville (UAH). It was national news and occurred the day after Medgar Evers was assassinated in his front yard in Jackson, Mississippi.

When others were afraid to move forward and stand up to local, state, or federal authorities, my dad refused to take "no" for an answer. When others feared prison or death, my dad moved forward into his destiny. He dreamed, weighed, measured, plotted, and then leaped into his possibilities and changed all of our fates forever. And when he landed, everyone cheered. Even though I wasn't born yet, I cheered too from wherever I was.

I was the kind of kid who would imagine that from my rites of passage, I would emerge heroic. Maybe I, too, would become a leader by popular demand after performing some incredible feat. In that regard, I could think of at least two different kinds of profound actions that, on the surface, could turn someone like me into a hero.

Perhaps I could save a life. This would be a safe choice, right? Later in my high school years, I would be at home, regretting my boring existence, and inspiration would hit. I would get in my car and drive around the community, looking for someone to save — some "damsel in distress." That is how most of the hero stories I knew went. But, damsels are sometimes hard to find.

In this day and age of frequent and regular global catastrophes and natural disasters, I do not advise this approach, not even for someone as hero-conscious as myself. Perhaps the safer course of heroism today is learning to find alignment between your physical existence and your spiritual potential. I discovered this more noble path only recently in my private maturation process. But nothing about me was authentically heroic when I was a kid.

THE COURAGE TO CHALLENGE MY STATUS QUO

Everyone in my entire household bore witness to the fact incredible dreams plagued me well into my teenage years. I dreamed of monsters, animals, demons, ghosts, witches, warlocks, and other masters and minions of the spiritual realm. I had these dreams so often that I became acquainted with many of these monsters and archetypes. I knew, on sight, which creatures I could trust and which ones would give chase at the drop of a dime. When I was first introduced to these characters, forces, energies, and possibilities, I was paralyzed with fear. But as I began to interact with them, over time, I slowly developed an aptitude to relate to them, interact with them, and even speak with them.

Eventually, I would grow to the point of being able to fight them and win decisively, sometimes even without injury. But initially, I suffered at their mercy. Soon, I learned to wield my power over these forces that were confined to my nighttime dreams.

Even though they were supernatural, these forces eventually followed the rules I imposed. But as a kid, these images followed me into consciousness and showed up in my vision but no one else's. They tormented me with their power and kept me humble so that I would never think more highly of myself than I should.

Given how my creative life has emerged, I am sure these dreams started on or even before my birth. By the time I was four and being chased by gory, towering monsters that somehow knew my name and my destiny, I developed the ability to shout at them and call for my dad to enter my space and fight them in a way I could not. I soon learned that when I shouted "Daddy" in my dream, everyone in the house could hear me.

Every time I shouted, Dad came running. Sometimes I would still be asleep running from the monsters when he arrived.

Other times I would be awake, certain that they had crossed the same chasm I did and were hiding in the darkness of my bedroom shadows, hoping my dad would forget to turn on the light.

WHAT I NEVER LEARNED TO SAY

Exposing my anxieties to my family was something I hated. I was irreparably embarrassed. My inability to manage my own dream life made me feel vulnerable. I was not emotionally secure in my skin. And even worse, I showed my brother, by my lack of dream control, that I was not yet the man I should be becoming. So, like the drunk who stumbles home after work, I was ashamed to talk about it the next day.

My dad told me that I had always been a different kid. And that even as a baby, I never wanted them to change my diapers. I guess I thought that since I had made the mess, I should be able to clean it up. Likewise, he told me that I came into the world attempting to find that same brand of independence in my own psychospiritual and emotional life.

Who would ever try to control their experience of supernatural forces? As years of orthodontic bills can attest, I spent far more than the normal amount of time with a pacifier. I could have gotten a graduate degree in self-comfort before starting kindergarten.

Even as a baby, I figured out how to rock my crib, which had no rocking capability. I would sit up on my legs, with my face in the pillow, and rock my body from side to side until I fell asleep, no matter how long it took.

Dad said he would leave me in my crib on one side of the room, even on the carpeted floor, only to return and find it on the other side. Still, to this day, when I wake up and try to go back to sleep, I use my foot to rock myself back to sleep. Old habits die hard.

Thank God my dad didn't seriously entertain the paranormal, or he may have assumed I needed an intervention or an exorcism. By the force of my imagination, I adopted a hyperaggressive spiritual lifestyle. But luckily, he understood that it was just how I constructed my reality to survive.

MY FEAR OF NOT BEING ACCEPTED

My dad's expectations for me grew with my childhood. He hoped that with ever-increasing responsibility, I could improve my standing in the family and community by staying safe, feeling grounded, and making better choices. He taught me the discipline of performance that would regulate my life.

Dad hoped that I would learn to manage my responses to what I could not control. I think this is the same standard that he used for himself. So, if it was good enough for him, it would certainly be good enough for me.

Or, so he thought.

I have since learned that during childhood, others thought the grass was much greener on my side. Most of my friends and colleagues could not imagine what they would trade for my life. But from my perspective, I lived life on autopilot with options I never chose.

I felt my success was my dad's and much more incidental

than intentional. My good fortune never felt like mine. What would I do with this consuming fire that burned within my imagination? Meanwhile, my true self was held imprisoned in my very soul.

But I have to admit that my dad's paradigm of external responsibility created a great life. It worked too well. Most of my family and friends thought I was incapable of doing anything wrong. That is until I got caught lying on the last day of 4th grade about having completed some dumb Social Studies assignment I had failed to turn in. I am still trying to live that down.

THE CHILDHOOD OF A DAREDEVIL

It was not easy growing up as the son of someone who so successfully negotiated his future and built a life, career, and family out of unfathomable possibilities. No wonder at least one of Dad's kids was destined to become a daredevil. I would have never described myself that way until recently, but there is no doubt that the title fits.

Being a daredevil is nothing I will ever prescribe for anyone else. But that is apparently how I naturally feel called to exist in the universe. As an unashamed risk-taker, I feel very much at home in my skin. I would not trade my life for anyone else's in history.

If too much time passes while doing nothing that requires considerable risk, I feel like a sponge drying out in the sun. I feel stagnant and unfulfilled, imagining that everyone else has all these options while I am stuck at the top of the universe with nowhere to go but down.

REJECTING SUFFERING AS THE PRICE OF LIVING FREE

Perhaps my excitement about being a daredevil comes from my attitude about suffering. That is the inference my dad was making about my decision to leave my job. He was concerned that until I prepared for a soft landing, quitting my job without a backup plan would most likely result in struggle.

But just because I struggle does not mean I have to suffer. This connects to the pie-in-the-sky mentality I mentioned in the last chapter. If you delay the pleasure of life for the afterlife, then all of life is suffering. But once my mortal life was threatened, I decided to make a different choice.

This is why I had to switch my paradigm and begin recording my journey through this series. In my paradigm, the experience of pain is par for the course. But who in their right mind would choose to suffer? Definitely, not me. So, this is how I responded.

COMPOSING A NEW STORY

I created *my* paradigm. I decided to experience a different story, one that put my interests and needs at the forefront and allowed me to let go of any story that no longer met my needs.

Instead, I choose to experience whatever comes on the path I choose to take. Whatever comes with it, that is what I will experience. But, on the other hand, if we are created in the image of the divine, where there is only light, why are we so afraid of suffering? Moreover, if we pay attention and see our lives from the highest vantage point, *how can we suffer?* This dilemma implicated my new paradigm and became a question I had to learn how to answer definitively.

As a kid, I only made the choices that were comfortable for my dad. Then, he had peace with me because he could easily predict my outcomes. But what was pleasurable for him was painful for me. I was suffering consequences for decisions that were never in my best interest.

But as a man, I slowly began to take the chances that were mine to take. This strained our relationship but moved the responsibility back to me. He told me often he wished I would defer to his judgment in important matters related to my life path. But the wiser I grew, the more I wanted to find my natural rhythm. According to him, I had become a rebel with a cause.

MANAGING UNPOPULAR CHOICES

My security was established in my father's plan. I was groomed to facilitate leadership in each of these spaces. Then, if anything ever happened, I could lead in their stead. Every moment was training for the next.

My natural orientation to this suffering question has always been fundamentally different from my dad's. Perhaps my security came more from the invisible than visible places. Having experienced all of the psychological and emotional turmoil of childhood, I fought the battles of the unknown and came out on top. I no longer feared what I could not see and became excited about what had not yet materialized.

I took my dad's calculations and came up with new results. But I did not appreciate how important this methodology was. In addition to all the spaces I was made to occupy for school and church, I was also established in places like the barbershop, the Boys and Girls Club, and Mama Anna's house.

Each of these spaces informed my worldview. They helped me frame the invisible forces I experienced. I found peace in uncomfortable situations. I did not have to control every aspect of my existence to feel secure. I learned to trust what I could not see to eventually have what I could not yet imagine.

As a result of this intention, I became secure and comfortable, not only in all spaces of Blackness but also in whiteness. Throughout our conservative southern experience, I learned to be content with little or much. So what others would consider suffering was not a big deal to me. I learned to relax and enjoy the ride, even the bumps along the way.

CHASTISEMENT TO REINFORCE OLD EXPECTATIONS

As I made mistakes, Dad corrected me in a way that was designed to reward my initiative and ambition while at the same time brutally chastising me. I was trained to consider my options carefully before making a choice.

Dad desperately wanted me to learn how to choose more wisely or position myself for the best outcomes available in any given situation. Whenever he would catch me moping in a lower version of myself, my dad would interrogate me for my good. *Son, what were you thinking? What possessed you to do that? Did you think I wouldn't find out? I always find out. That's what dads do. They find things out.*

So, you may ask, how did that system work after moving out of my parents' house? Did those strategies and disciplines carry over after high school?

They did. College was a breeze.

After high school, our maturation process continued as my siblings and I went to college. I chose Georgia Tech, and they chose me. But my dad feared that Atlanta was outside of his sphere of influence.

THE NEW LAND OF THE FAMILIAR

My brother was already at Auburn, and that is where my dad felt safe with my future. At Auburn, the most likely co-conspirators in his process were demanding professors and Greek-lettered organizations. Although neither of my parents pledged, my siblings and I seized that opportunity. We secured further social and emotional credentials in the process.

My dad was not wrong about Auburn. In fact, it was the perfect place for me. But it was not my choice. Atlanta would equip me with options that even my dad never considered. But he never embraced the sociology of a bustling city. He thought there was a greater chance I would be more corrupted by the anonymity than equipped by the possibility. So even though he was right, I resented that I could not make this discovery on my own.

I attribute most of my college success to the brotherhood I shared with Greek-lettered organizations. I was fortunate to join the ranks of Kappa Alpha Psi Fraternity, Incorporated. Their rituals continued the rites of passage I had begun in childhood. Those traditions tapped into the collective unconscious of pre-American societies and Indigenous communities on all continents.

SURVIVING RITES OF PASSAGE

Indigenous cultures have mandated rituals of passage for thousands, if not tens of thousands of years. Childhood is given up in exchange for intangible possibilities. Once the community agrees that you are mature and officially done with childhood, you can face all things both in the known and unknown worlds.

This initiation process further elaborated on those barbershop conversations I had as a kid. And it's a good thing they did. There are aspects of my character that I had refused to touch before joining my fraternity. For example, I was often described as extremely "hard-headed." That meant I was stubborn and often insisted on having my way, even in the face of adverse circumstances for myself and those around me.

And just as designed, the initiation process was very public and unapologetic. It pointed out character flaws and exposed each of them to light. On more than one occasion, I was warned that the elders of my fraternity would simply refuse my entry into the fraternity.

I had to figure out how to confront my flaws and respond affirmatively and decisively. This was one of the most important goals of the process. I subjected myself to initiation for my personal betterment and the resulting development of the fraternal bond and the chapter's reputation at the University.

Once I developed my new paradigm into spiritual practice, I found this exposure technique to be an essential part of the basic motif of the hero's journey. In this process, I was expected to leave my childhood identity and home in one form and find energy, life, and sources to transform me so that I could finally return home in my higher form.

This awakening enables me to teach those same skills to my family and community. These lessons and opportunities manifest in both the physical and spiritual realms. Then later, I will return home to assume leadership in those spaces so that younger kids may develop and follow in those same footsteps.

PERSONALITY FLAWS AND PUBLIC TRANSFORMATION

But there are more than a few contemporary challenges with this fraternal approach. Personal transformation never completes itself in a group process. A person's character must be transformed on the individual level, even on the quantum level.

Many unresolved childhood issues are strong enough to evade the transformation inferred by the ceremony. In those instances, I have often learned the hard way that wherever they show up, those unresolved issues of character must be acknowledged, addressed, and accommodated. Exposed and often embarrassed, I was, nevertheless, inspired to pursue the interventions available to me.

Several issues that evaded my public transformation were connected to my unique family experience and blood ties. Most importantly, I discovered that there was trauma from my parents that was passed on to me. As a Black American whose ancestors were enslaved, this should be no surprise to me or anyone else, but it was. I thought that by virtue of my education and personal success, I could escape those generational curses that coursed through my veins from the time of my entry onto this plane.

As a result of those traumas, my spiritual foundation naturally builds on top of shaky ground. I am easily triggered by anxiety and worry. If left to my own devices, these issues can develop into emotional pitfalls that strongly resemble depression and isolation.

I can easily begin to doubt my worth and unique reason for existence. And before long, I can forget all of the advances and successes my family and I have experienced. I can lose track of all of the joys and gifts that more than balance my life.

But that is what trauma does — it makes you forget the tools you have to fight. These traumas tend to hide in the unconscious and wait until the threat of being exposed passes. Where I have insisted on holding on to unsolved issues in my character, these issues hide within me and threaten to trigger me into a lower version of myself at any moment.

THE EGO AND THE SOUL'S NEED TO HEAL

Your public persona never recovers from buried scars.

And how could it be when you did not even know that those scars were there?

Families often fail to discuss difficult things. Just "give it to God" and keep moving like nothing's wrong. You have to learn to do this later work alone. You can face any difficulty life has shown you. But you cannot heal until you allow yourself to hurt.

But you are an expert in presenting well. That makes the work of healing all the more difficult. The work you needed was never superficial but foundational. You will have to learn how to restore your foundation. You will have to learn to deliver yourself from evil.

This is not work that I even heard about until recently. All I knew was school, church, family, and career. But those spaces were not designed to facilitate what remains unaddressed.

The inner work is different. Here is where you learn to align with your pre-traumatic self. This work only happens in invisible places. This private work required to heal is much more arduous than any public work could be.

These inner private issues show up clearly when you are in safe spaces. There, you may pursue the necessary path of transformation. Then, finally, you can show up again in public with a solid spiritual core. In that capacity, the ceremony of graduation becomes a symbol of the work already done behind closed doors. Although my lived example has been challenging, I have been the test case. I know that every soul is capable of finding the hiding hero. Regardless of what you think about yourself, you have the ability to be heroic in this way.

By virtue of your very existence, you are born a hero. Even as a tiny embryo shaped in water, you developed the capacity to survive and thrive. You developed and grew in unimaginable circumstances. Until the maturation process was fully realized, you were sheltered by your mother.

You then moved out into the world, outside of the protection of your old routine and former lifestyle. You learned to live outside of your small controlled living space. You transformed into a being who no longer needed those rules to survive. But survival was never enough for your inner hero. You learned to move, breathe, and pursue life independently, uniquely, and wonderfully.

And look at you now!

This is the story of the original hero's journey. Nature determined this common journey would be the same throughout the universe. Although we share this common history, our journeys are individual. Your successful matriculation remains your responsibility.

Nature also confers on us the image and memory of the journeys of our foreparents and collective communities. This is the source of generational blessings and curses. According to some stories, this birth process confers on us the image of a Creator-Designer. This equips us with early meaning and possibility. In some traditions, this image carries spiritual potential. Cooperation equips us to occupy the space we were created to hold.

Our ignorance about our true nature and existence creates a misalignment with our reality. Our minds experience suffering because it is how we are out of touch with our reality. In other words, all of this suffering is created in the mind but is not our actual experience. It is like watching a scary movie and forgetting to distinguish our thoughts from the images projected on the screen.

Most pain and all suffering warn us that we are misaligned. So, it is not a good idea to pursue a life without pain. Pain is a feedback mechanism that is designed for our self-preservation. So when we touch something hot, we quickly withdraw our hands.

Pain is in our design and is given for our protection. Mind-created suffering functions in the same way. It only arises when we refuse to let go of what no longer serves us. We should only hold the rituals, myths, and stories that align with our experience of reality.

I remember when I was stuck with regret about a past breakup. I rehearsed statements like, "I'll never be happy without her." At first, the pain of losing someone seems unbearable. Without this mantra, there is no internal story to turn pain into suffering. So, as with time, pain passes, and we eventually move on.

Life can turn into hurt in a given moment. But that is part of the maturation process. Then, through community and ritual, we can ground and realign our bodies. And return to ourselves with freedom, joy, and love. The best thing I have ever done was submit myself to my natural healing process — something I had always tried to avoid. Looking back, I realize that I tried to skip this process. As a result, I found myself in a cycle, experiencing pain over and over again. But now, I am on the other side of my transformation. I am not worried about whether I will make it out alive. I accept responsibility for my own experience. Now, I realize that only my perspective makes any of these sensations real.

Regardless of what happens, I know it's gonna be good.

Mama Anna

These observations are new to you but not to your bloodline. If your ancestors had not been able to find good even in the vicious cycle of disenfranchisement and oppression, they would have all jumped from those ships in the Atlantic to never be heard from again. But you are here on the earth because you are a survivor.

My life has sometimes been filled with challenge and pain. I'm so grateful for all of it, and I wouldn't change a single thing.

Hareesh Saurabh

We are going to ask our egos and our personas to find a quiet place to reflect and digest while our essence, our souls, and our unconscious begins to remind us that we are more than our public presence. That there is a wisdom buried inside us that has been patiently waiting to be invited to the table. And now that we are here together, we are going to begin to create a space for the duration of time that we are sitting with this text and with these thoughts with this agenda before us.

Chauncey McGlathery

AFFIRMATIONS

I am endowed with the creative power to make choices about my experience of the world.

I am aware of the freedoms I am born with as a human being.

I am as content to experience pleasure as I am to experience pain.

I am empowered to deal with life as it actually is, not as I wish it were.

I am secure in my flaws and humble in my strengths.

I am confident that I can manage any situation in which I find myself.

CHAPTER THREE
MASTERING

Always remember your focus determines your reality.
George Lucas

The bridge between knowledge and skill is practice. The bridge between skill and mastery is time.
Jim Bouchard

In Chapter Two, I outlined my pace of survival. I shared the challenges I had to overcome in my head in order to move in my body. I shared how embarrassed I was to be vulnerable, even with my loved ones. Finally, I describe the process of my soul seizing power from my ego.

Using my survival as an example, you can choose a similar path. Create spaces so that you can become comfortable with your insecurities. Find opportunities to share your vulnerability with those you care about. And don't be surprised when they start doing the same. Make room for the change of responses you will get from those who think they know you. Get excited about becoming a higher version of yourself than you have ever imagined.

In this third chapter, I will share the developmental stage of mastering. I will describe how the best vocational decisions are sometimes hidden at first glance. I will share how to navigate cultural restrictions to get to where you belong. I will conclude by assuring you that the peace you gain as you vibrate on a higher plane will be worth more than the price you pay.

CHOOSING MY VOCATION

By my junior year of college, I needed to upgrade my vocational choice. Engineering did not seem to have the potential to launch me into my destiny. But what was I going to be if not an engineer just like my dad?

I knew Dad desired to be an attorney. Being a pastor before my siblings and I were born, he felt called to help communities become empowered and enfranchised. While at Auburn, I also became a licensed and ordained minister. But my love of spiritual work was much more focused on work outside the building. I was doubtful that pastoring could satisfy my internal call to action.

A law practice could make a difference in the lives of the community members that I loved so dearly. I would attend Howard University School of Law, then move back to Auburn and start a solo practice. At least, that was the plan.

Ironically, at Howard, I had a law professor who matriculated under apartheid in South Africa. He did not think I should have been admitted to Howard at all. As he explained it, apartheid was like Jim Crow in its social enforcement of cultural boundaries. And he believed my skin was too dark for me to possess the intellectual prowess I needed to do well in law school. In fact, during a lecture, he informed me that I was one of those who were not historically allowed to pursue any type of graduate degree. In the Americas, the Jim Crow rule that enforced this colorist restriction was called "the paper bag test," he explained. Since this was all new to me, I called my dad later that night.

ME: *Dad, what's the paper bag test?*

DAD: *The what?*

ME: *The paper bag test? My constitutional law professor told me that back in the day, you couldn't get into graduate school unless your complexion was—*

DAD: *Oh yeah. Lighter than a paper bag.*

ME: *So that was a real thing?*

DAD: *Of course, son. How do you think I was able to do so well at NASA?*

ME: *What do you mean?*

DAD: *As a result of my skin, I had options. I had choices. And I was exposed to a higher level of education and opportunity than my darker-skinned counterparts. So I could do whatever I wanted. To a certain point, of course. But that's why I am the leader in various aspects of life, from work to church.*

ME: *Church?*

DAD: *Yeah. Those rules applied across the board, not only in business but even in the cotton fields, even during slavery. How do you not know this?*

THE EGO AND SOCIETAL RESTRICTIONS

Even at the mecca of Historically Black Universities & Institutions, I had to be on my guard again. This felt more like Alabama than Huntsville ever did. So, I had to change my entire approach to law school. When I got back to campus, I looked again at the wall of framed graduating class pictures hung throughout the hallway.

It never dawned on me to look to see how dark or light-skinned the graduates in the black and white pictures were. But now that I looked, I could see the effective application of this restrictive social practice. Some of the graduates were even passable as white. Almost everyone was noticeably lighter-skinned. And I was darker than almost all of them.

Did all my professors still think like Jim Crow Southerners? Did my colleagues think I wouldn't make the grade?

I decided to conduct a social experiment. I launched a campaign to demonstrate that I was at least as competent and skilled as everyone else. My ego demanded it under my childhood paradigm. So, in every campaign and every trial I competed, I won.

I needed to show them what I should not have had to tell them. I could rise to whatever standard of excellence required. At the time, it was what I liked most about myself. I had the ability to overcome any challenge. I preferred to shift the odds in favor of the underdog. Only this time, instead of cheering from the stands, I would be in the game. This was the fulfillment of my early childhood dreams. Only instead of running with a ball, I argued with a briefcase.

And I took no prisoners.

Before I became Editor-In-Chief of the Law Journal, I became president of the class, going up against another lighter-skinned brother, much to the dismay of many of my fellow law schoolmates. As it turns out, I had much more of my dad in me than I ever thought I did. There was this passion inside me that ignited whenever someone tried to withhold what I felt belonged to me.

If I had never learned about the paper bag test, I would have never thought about becoming class president. And then, when the moot court competition came around, I would not have given it a second thought if I had not done well.

Once I suspected that my colleagues thought I did not belong, I had to go for the jugular. With no expectation of winning, I prepared and took off my jacket after the first round. I was getting ready to go back to living because I had demonstrated, even in that first round, that I was never to be underestimated.

Then, they called the name of the 16 finalists out of the entire school of over 400. I was one of them. I had to put my jacket back on and get ready for the next round. The next publication of names would be a list of the final four. So I said, "Well, now I'm sure they know." Again, getting ready to leave, they announced the names, and I was one of them. The final part of the competition would happen a few days later, and this time, the entire school would be there. At this point, I was just having fun.

OPPORTUNITIES WITHIN EVERY OBSTACLE

By advancing in this competition, I realized that there were always great opportunities lurking within every obstacle. The only question was whether or not I was willing to put forth the intention. Would I seize those opportunities and turn them into victories? Soon, I would find that this choice mattered in grad school and the real world.

Everybody gathered on that night; I think it was a Monday. By this time, I was the only Black male remaining in the competition, and the word had gotten out that I was coming into my own. While making my arguments, the student body would often laugh or applaud something I had said.

COMPOSING A NEW STORY

Every once in a while, I would catch a glimpse of one of my professors, who would smile with pride as I argued the moot court case. I was back on stage, very much like I had been my whole life. Something inside me was explosive. I was learning to inspire, challenge, and change myself to be better than before. And in the process, I found my calling to be a light in the darkness. And in the cold, callous world of apathy and cynicism, I was a flame.

However, my battle wins set me up to lose the war. When I lost the beacon of leadership I had in my dad, I fell under the impossible weight of grief. The paradigm that fed my ego failed me in my time of crisis. And I desperately needed to revisit my childhood stories and find a replacement for my purpose-driven life.

GRIEF AS A MOTIVATION FOR CHANGE

Grief employs an essential place of our emotional being. Especially in times like these, we see how easily life is prematurely snatched. The modern-day lynching deaths of brothers like Ahmaud Arbery and George Floyd show this all too well. Grief can cause us to lose our breath if we do not know how to return to our center.

My community has the unfortunate distinction of becoming experts in managing the energy that comes with grief. Whenever Jim Crow rears its ugly head, we go into a familiar mode of rationalizing the senseless. If we chose to respond to hate and injustice with rage, we would be well within our rights.

But mastery is not about rights; it is about our love for ourselves. Not the duties we have to anyone and anything outside of ourselves. Although I am tempted to resent the feelings that death brings to me, my perspective on grief has evolved as I grow older and wiser.

Now, death allows me to experience and express love through grief. In death, I reflect on my mortality and the sensitive nature in which my life remains in existence. It is critical that we do all that we can to ensure that life continues to be beautiful for all who will come after us.

Like characters in a common story, heroes from all over the world experience palpable grief. However, we do not want to remain or abide or dwell indefinitely in that place for too long. We don't want to abide in sorrow, despair, hopelessness, or powerlessness.

MASTERING PRIVATE CHALLENGES

In rewriting our stories, we employ language that honors the hope within us. There is still breath in us, and we need to find what that breath is in the universe to do. We are capable of a more perfect transformation than we have seen with our own eyes.

With this new age, we have a new level of consciousness. During the worst of our mundane sorrows, we can access our greatest hopes and dreams. We are equipped to do more than survive this terrible age. Oh, we can master it. Death is not our end but a twist in the plot of our existence here.

It was not until the last few years of my life that I felt comfortable and even excited about addressing internal challenges. I can return to the barbershop with my nephews or younger neighbors. I can help them value rituals as a powerful grounding experience in life.

Now, they will begin to discover their initiation process. Next, they will learn to survive, and then, they will grow into mastery. They may never become heroes in the grand sense of redeeming society. But I can help them develop the necessary competence to make that journey for themselves.

This mastery stage is one of the most daunting aspects of the journey. Instead of valiant charging ahead and fighting, many succumb to their low-frequency urges to follow the rules. Either we hide and shrink, or we become preoccupied with our work as a measure of success. We may find ourselves in a stalemate, but we do not have to stay there for long.

Living in a self-constructed reality, I held up my guard most of the time. Eventually, when I grew tired of masquerading as something I was not, I would slip from acting and cower and submit to the basest of my primal instincts. But eventually, I decided to wake up from my preoccupation and reconsider the question I had all along.

What is the reason for my existence on this planet? What was the purpose of being placed here in the first place?

BREATH AND THE SOUL OF THE HERO

I struggled with that question while hearing the words, "I Can't Breathe." These words have represented a collective but often unspoken effect.

"You have taken from me my ability to choose life. You have robbed me of my ability to be a living soul."

Although I reject their premise, for George Floyd, those words were prophetic. He acknowledged the plot to overrule his choice to live. Then, after he made his declaration, we saw that word manifest in death.

I cannot accept those words as any universal truth. No simple plot is more powerful than the universe's original intention. The flow of love on the earth will sustain the continuation of life until it decides otherwise.

EXPERIENCE LOVE WHEN YOU SPEAK LIFE

My purpose is to speak life into myself. What are we declaring on ourselves, and what can we affirm? How can we shift the narrative, shift the consciousness, and change the conversation? We have the power to ride over treacherous storms and malevolent intentions. The ability to choose our path is our greatest resource.

You can influence the earth and your role in it. So, we should declare that "We can and we will!" Rather than, "I can't and I won't." We cannot ever let anyone find us looking outward for either our life or peace. It is critical that we recognize that we have this breath, this ability, and this conscious power to live and move forward.

In the Genesis story, the writer explains that the reason the decision was made to breathe life and turn humans into living souls is so that we can then have dominion and power over the rest of this creation. So why would I, who the universe has given power, forfeit my ability to be myself in word or deed?

MASTER THE AUTHENTIC POWER OF YOUR INNER HERO

The first weapon we learn to master is the tongue. A judge in a courtroom declares a thing, and it becomes. Our words are the clearest technology to channel the power we have. What you confess, speak out, and declare has a frequency and a vibration. Your words ignite energy within a thing to accomplish its purpose. Why not speak over yourself?

But when we do not know our words have power, we may declare that "we can't breathe." Even if I get justice or peace or breath, I know it has not come from me because I have forfeited my power to bring it about.

It must have come to me externally without my input, influence, or participation. What then happens to my authority? I give it up, and I am now out of alignment with my role or destiny in the Universe.

Consider the plot of the movie, The Matrix. In the movie, the hero, Nero, is confronted by Morpheus, who, in essence, tells Nero that he has the option of pills to take. One will allow him to go back to sleep and forget that he and Morpheus had ever met. While the other will disconnect him from everything, he knew but would lead him to his destiny and give him autonomy to choose his life for better or for worse.

For the last decade or so, I have been persuaded that the concepts of what we call "good" and "evil" are more about our perspectives than they are about nature. So, where do I think these social structures come from? Our myths and our stories.

It is no surprise that the plot of The Matrix affected the culture the way it did. It tapped into the narrative from our collective unconscious that says, "We are trapped in a mundane existence." We are successful, but it no longer means anything. Surely, there must be more.

ENGAGE THE DREAM MACHINE

Ironically, my first experience of this plot was not in the movie but one of the dreams from my childhood. In the dream, I met a wise, old guru who eventually showed me something amazing — the dream machine. He gave me the following choice:

> *If you choose to push this button on this machine, any one of three things could happen. 1) You can experience all of the joys you can imagine. 2) You will also meet the fears of your scariest nightmares. 3) If you push it, you will forget you pushed it and be plunged into a world of infinite possibility. However, if you choose not to push the button, you will wake up, and nothing will change.*

At this point in the dream, I woke up in a cold sweat. There was no way I was going back to sleep. Given the odds of being plunged into boundless hope and pleasure on the one hand and boundless suffering on the other, what would I choose?

This is Adam and Eve all over again.

Was this a trick, or was this real? Did I really have the ability to change my life so that my "regular" life could be a thing of the past? And, if I could, was I willing to take the chance that I was not going to make everything so much worse?

Having thought about this choice over the years, I reached two very important conclusions. First of all, we all have this choice. We all get to decide how long we will live the same life we have always had. Every day that we wake up and start the same routine as the day before, we make this choice.

Second of all, I have discovered that once we come to this realization, there is only one choice left to be made. Whoever finds themselves in that situation will eventually always take the red pill. Just ask Adam. We always eat the forbidden fruit, and we always push the button. The only question is not whether you will do it, but rather, how long will you wait?

THE QUEST TO FIND HAPPINESS

We think we would be happy having every need met perfectly without raising a finger. Our history disproves this fact time and time again. Only by allowing all the possibilities within consciousness will we ever be content to exist in this universe. One guru, Hareesh Saurabh, says that *"it is only by granting the whole world its perfect freedom to be exactly as it wants to be that any one of us can truly be free."*

One difficulty found as I have attempted to master this dilemma is my consumerism. The nature of my materialistic culture oriented me to the most base levels of reality. By continually identifying myself only by my physical senses and moods, I appealed to my lowest frequencies. I reduced myself to a creature capable of only experiencing life and reality at that surface level.

I simply forgot to relate to any level of depth. Totally ignored in my response was my true soul dimension. Here is the place in my body where all my stories originate. Here is where the cosmic DNA of all of humanity is encoded. But I choose to engage like a hero and discover this deeper existence. Only then would I master the test through great trial and perseverance.

SECURITY BEYOND THE LAND OF FAMILIAR

As a kid, I lived behind walls secured by my parents. Behind locks, I was tucked safely away from all hurt, harm, and danger. I never had to confront any of life's puzzling realities. My dad and mom did that on my behalf.

I perfected only the lessons that they filtered to me. They were not able to teach me what they had never learned. I never chose to see most of what was even out there. Because I was not engaging in the universe for myself, I hardly ever felt brave.

Whether it was a teacher, parent, coach, pastor, mentor, or guru, it was easier for someone else to do that work of perceiving and filtering to me only what I needed to know. The rest of it was garbage that I discarded without a second thought. But in those years of transition from childhood, I had no one to filter. Outside of those constructed walls, I felt overwhelmed, disoriented, confused, and lost. Even though I complained, I was comfortable with what I was shown.

But when I finally decided to move into my own space, I began considering what I had never known. This was a very difficult transition from the security of my childhood home. I was accustomed to having authority in my life to define reality for me.

At first, I recreated the security I had with my parents. I reconstructed the same walls I had come to know as a child. Then, hoping to find more joy and pleasure in what I had never been exposed to, I would sneak outside the barriers and engaged in the universe with no filter.

This phenomenon of filtering has been happening in our culture from the very beginning. M. Night Shyamalan explored this narrative perfectly in his feature film *The Village*. Through stories, histories, and legends, we created myths to protect us from what we thought was "out there." This safety mechanism informed our perspective for several millennia.

I can also see that I replicated in my life what humans have done since the beginning. When I could not readily address the universe's age-old questions, I stopped looking for answers. When I could not answer why I was here or my purpose, I simply chose to disengage. My coping strategy was to make myself busy. But this distraction almost cost me my life.

As of a few years ago, I have fully embarked on this journey. None of the old barriers protect me anymore from experiencing the world as it is. Now that I engage with reality fully and completely, everything has changed. My ability to connect with new ideas and new communities is beyond my wildest dreams.

John Lennon said, "Life is what happens to you when you are busy making other plans." I would like to modify that thought:

Life is what you miss while you are busy looking.

But once I acknowledged my tendency of preoccupation, I knew I must return to my journey. Just because you wake up in a bunker does not mean you have to die there.

MAINTAIN YOUR SPACE OF ILLUMINATION

After the very hard work of balancing yourself and your family, a space can be created with choices you have never known. By personal and public illumination, you can choose the outcomes you need to make your house a home.

It is easy to come to this step too quickly. No stage of this hero's journey is as linear as this layout might suggest. Some aspects may be ready for mastery, while others are still in the discovery stage. But once at the level of mastery, the hero must first acknowledge the pitfalls that threaten survival. Then, they can also teach these concepts and mentor others who are also coming along behind.

The lessons you read in books like this are fantastic if you have a great imagination. They can easily give you comfort or peace in chaotic times like these. I overestimated my adult readiness in my twenties. But theories and assumptions are not reality. It is easy to think you are wiser than you are before life happens to you.

Here is another mistake we often make. You cannot understand marriage until you are married. You do not know what it means to handle childbirth, divorce, or the death of a parent until these things happen to you. Then, when it is your turn, you will find out exactly what you are made of. And the universe and the ancestors will be watching as you fight your way through.

We will hold a space that will finally affirm us at a quantum level that nothing about us, nothing having to do with us, our hopes, or our destinies, has ever been more possible than it is right now. We are going to slowly begin to raise our hands with our expectations. We begin to celebrate that all we hoped would be is waiting to meet us at the point of new decisions, new opportunities, new possibilities, and new potentials because finally, we are equipping ourselves to know the greatest truth of ourselves that the half about our journeys has not yet been told.

Chauncey McGlathery

I'm not telling you to make the world better because I don't think that progress is necessarily part of the package. I'm just telling you to live in it. Not just to endure it, not just to suffer it, not just to pass through it, but to live in it. To look at it. To try to get the picture. To live recklessly. To take chances. To make your work and take pride in it. To seize the moment."

Joan Didion

AFFIRMATIONS

I am aware of the power I have to acknowledge and accept every aspect of myself.
I am confident in my ability to adapt, evolve, and change to bring out the very best version of myself that I ever imagined.
I am committed to confessing my opportunities for growth in order to live openly, honestly, and authentically.
I am convinced that my best has not yet been imagined even by me.

I am pleased to celebrate the successes of my neighbors and to mourn their losses as a vested member of the human race. I am determined to be the example of intention and consistently loving energy in order to have the strongest impact on my family and community.

CHAPTER FOUR
BELONGING

The world is hard for everyone but particularly if you look different or love different.

Joy Oladokun

The two most important days in your life are the day you are born and the day you find out why.

Mark Twain

In Chapter Three, I outlined my adult pursuit of mastery. I shared the pitfalls I fell into en route to finding my footing. I shared how I used vocational success to soothe my ego. Finally, I described how I adjusted my expectations in my newly illuminated life of consciousness.

Using my mastery as a model, you can follow a similar thread. You can expect to find happiness on the edge of a life of adventure. You can be secure as you equip yourself to battle against the fears that arise within you. You can embrace the pain of your experience as food for the journey. And your level of happiness can increase with the difficulty of every stage.

In this fourth chapter, I will describe the developmental stage of belonging. I will describe how I changed my worldview and paradigm. I will conclude by describing the challenges of renegotiating your identity and how to respond to the pushback you may receive from your friends and neighbors.

BELONGING IN BROKENNESS

The most effective activism is awakening your true nature. When you have awakened, you learn to live in harmony with your complete environment. You never use your choices to resist the natural flow because you realize that you are the natural flow.

Everything we do in activism is merely an attempt to compensate for the fact humanity remains asleep. Thus, our efforts fail in inverse proportion to the consciousness of those we attempt to activate. Everyone in every place is attempting to do the same thing. They are living according to their perception of reality. They are trying to maximize their freedom and happiness from their experience of the Universe within them.

My family was no exception to this rule. Culturally, we were considered Black at school but not *really* "Black" at all. *You're not like the others,* I've heard it said. *Your culture is excellence,* my dad could have said. *That's who you are at school.*

I heard a line in my new favorite show, Succession, that grabbed me. "He only likes you because you're broken," the actor said. I had to pause the stream immediately when I heard it. As profound as this sentiment was, it sounded so familiar. This is my experience of the typical response to my cultural expression. Society only likes me when I am broken.

This idea made me search myself and my experiences for references. I recall how fragile I became after a few notable disappointments in my thirties. In failure, certain people and institutions, from my church to my healthcare providers, seemed to latch on to me. They were only interested when there was something broken for them to hang on to. Here is the news flash. *If I had to be broken to get your attention, I would rather live without it.*

STORIES IN BLACK AND WHITE

In Chapter Two, I referenced the pie-in-the-sky worldview I held in my youth. Again, this says that good people should expect good results. And bad people should expect bad results. Of course, I knew that this black-and-white way of thinking was ridiculous from my research and life experience. But still, I would not let it go.

Having been woefully disappointed in others as a kid, I decided, like my dad, that I could do it all by myself. I resolved never to take anyone else's advice or help. I enforced my discipline, which left no room for error. Nobody knew how rough I made my life as a kid. I quietly suffered anxiety, bitterness, and regret about my process but could not stop it.

This binary framework meant there was a relationship between sadness and failure that was inseparable. But relating happiness with impending success was disproven time and time again. But because I thought I was on the "right" side of this algorithm, I did not think it mattered if I upgraded my thinking.

The old way was wrong but was too comfortable to let go. It allowed me to think I was assured success because I thought I was good. I never questioned whether there was another way to experience the universe. My life seemed to follow perfectly in line with this thinking early on. I felt I deserved the peace that came with this simple worldview because of the very wild and traumatic inner spirit life I had as a child.

Then, having grown up, I was desperately hoping to replicate it in the lives of my loved ones. When it brought me success, I doubled down. I became the most miserable version of a success story you have ever seen.

"I really, really want to build a culture and a world that invites people in instead of pushing them out. It's called a "calling-in culture."

Loretta J. Ross

MY MESSIAH COMPLEX

I refused to reflect on what was going on inside me. I preferred to keep the spotlight on everyone else. I blocked my ability to share my heart with my loved ones. Instead, I barricaded myself and focused on who and what was around me.

I was unaware that I chose these brass tactics, and even less aware of their lack of effectiveness. Constantly, I would throw out little tests of character. Always challenging everyone around me, I was standing by, waiting to jab.

What are you gonna do now that you're in trouble? What are you ever gonna come up with now? I thought they would continue to be miserable failures until they let me swoop in and save them. That was the love language with which I was raised.

But even when I should have become a man, I refused to put away these childish things. I hung on to my old way of thinking because it was convenient. I held on to the view that those who succeeded worked harder and deserved success. Everyone else failed because there was something fundamentally wrong with their approach.

I used to believe that Black people struggled by their own choice. They refused to conform to European standards and had not committed themselves to excellence. I thought I was reading the world through realistic eyes, but now I know I was trapped in colonial thinking.

I had been educated with an oppressive pedagogy. I was trapped in a Civil War worldview. I was reprojecting the horrors of systemic racism. And I thought I could not be racist by virtue of my skin color.

RECONSTRUCTING IDENTITY

I worked hard to avoid being mistaken for any stereotypes. I invented a new type that I thought had no cultural baggage. I became obsessed with success, education, and career.

I believed I was worthy of love because of what I had accomplished. This narcissistic performance was celebrated in the myths of my childhood. It was poison in my well, hiding shame with celebration and praise.

One of the righteous virtues I held closely was my unadulterated disappointment with the human experiment. As a perfectionist, I knew life would not get any better for so many. I resented friends, neighbors, and colleagues because of their plight.

The more successful I got, the worse this ideology weighed me down. That is tragic because I had always loved my friends as family. I was always desperate to see them all succeed. But I blamed them while I failed to adequately care for myself.

Even though it cost my peace, the sacrifice was worth it. I would take private credit for their advances while excusing my distance from them. After all, what else comes with power but responsibility?

Why was I responsible for others' choices? No one's lack of success reflected anything about me. It was my fault that I was so disappointed. No one needed help more than me.

PERFECTIONISM AS DEFENSE MECHANISMS

But I was blind to my shortcomings. It was easy for me to focus on what others needed to do. Because I had traveled so far down this road, certainly I had passed the point of no return.

Hadn't I?

I was desperate to show excellence in my community. I was committed to challenging the many perpetuated stereotypes in our popular culture. Unfortunately, some of these lower frequencies in our culture had become so famous that many assumed these ridiculed stereotypes were true.

THE GOOD NEGRO

This lesson was never more clear than at Boston College. An older Black colleague asked me to decide what kind of scholar I would be. He thought that I should be grateful to be a part of the faculty. He said that I would need to manage their expectations of my "style."

Either I would be a "good negro" like Martin Luther King, Jr., or I would be a "bad negro" like Malcolm X. All I could do was shake my head in astonishment. *Negro, what did you just say to me?*

I had to explain this conflict to my Boston College undergraduates. So I added it to the syllabus in my *Rhythm & Blues and the Irony of the Negro Artist* class. It was one of the most enlightening conversations we ever had.

These students had no reference for this kind of conversation. Therefore, I had to first lay the groundwork for these social constructions. Then, they would understand the gravity of this brother's miseducation.

AMERICAN MINSTRELS

I introduced them to stereotypes that were prevalent in southern lore and culture. I explained the time when minstrels entertained the world. Trauma-ridden caricatures owned our popular culture. Their tropes celebrated prejudices that are still alive until this day.

One of the most famous of these minstrel types was Zip Coon. Coon was well-dressed, with exaggerated lapels wider than his shoulders. Another type was Jim Crow, the big-shooed field hand. With hay in his hair, he spoke with a very slow drawl to emphasize his rural roots.

To be a Negro in this country and to be relatively conscious is to be in a state of rage almost, almost all of the time — and in one's work. And part of the rage is this: It isn't only what is happening to you. But it's what's happening all around you.

James Baldwin

The three remaining characters are "Cute Pickanny," "Old Darky," and, of course, "Mammy." Whereas the persona of Kanye West would resemble the Jim Crow type, Lil Nas X would resemble the type of Zip Coon. Once I included these modern-day examples, all of a sudden, we were all on the same page.

For people who have never belonged to a group that included Black people, these stereotypes may be all they ever knew. By extension, I feared that when strangers met me for the first time, their only question would be if I was like Zip Coon or Jim Crow.

I had never been confronted with this simple reduction of identity. It never raised its ugly head in my youth. But I always expected this kind of problem in Alabama. When confronted with this level of ignorance in Boston, I had to stop and count to ten.

THE INSECURE PROFESSIONAL

I had always embraced confrontation as a courageous virtue. But for my older Black colleague, this was a vice. He feared I would jeopardize the favor he found as a go-along-to-get-along professional.

This gentleman was a member of my father's generation. He had never experienced success by rocking the boat. He only feared being fired for being hypercritical. Surely he had seen Blacks on that campus fired for their refusal to conform. And his fear was not misplaced.

What was progressive for me was threatening for my colleague. If I had not transformed just a few years ago, I would continue to be as miserable as he. Before awakening to my colonial baggage, I, too, was imprisoned by the stories I embraced when I thought myself to be infallible.

THE CHOICE OF PROGRESS

I am learning from the trauma within my heart. I still carry vestiges of perfectionism within my body and in my muscle memory. Progress for me has come with intention and ritual. Whereas failure is often public, these wins are usually private and personal.

What I never considered under my old paradigm was the choice I had all along. And some of the Black people I had looked down on were far more mature than me. In choosing their own culture, they had chosen to represent themselves authentically, which was different from what the European standard suggests. They had confused me the same way I had confused my colleague.

I soon joined the ranks of the politely dismissed faculty, but not before I forever changed that culture. My students have gone on to become strong advocates for progress. And that is exactly what their most authentic selves demanded. I was never more excited than when I later discovered the activism of my students. They organized the protest on campus when Trayvon Martin was killed.

When you ask people to give up hate, then you need to be there for them when they do.

C.T. Vivian

WHEN THEY GO LOW, WE GO HIGH

On this high frequency, authenticity has a profound meaning to my community. Blacks in America prove the human spirit will always prevail. And that necessity can turn mothers into matriarchs.

When we could not drive, we invented new styles of walking. When we were forced to eat low on the hog, we created the delicacy of chitterlings. When we were only worthy to receive rotten peaches, we created the cobbler. When given scraps instead of the finer fabrics for sewing, we created a new fashion that first showed up as quilts.

My ancestors' virtues looked and felt very different from my old paradigm. On the east coast, where I could dialogue about these ideas much easier, emphasis was placed on the style of Blackness as excellent and beautiful. I had not learned until my later years to appreciate and prefer our style.

THE REBIRTH OF BELONGING

In pursuit of transformation, you can revisit your vulnerabilities. Brokenness is something that you can embrace, process, and learn from. I suspect that you and I are born into some supernatural design. Otherwise, how can you explain your role in this vast Universe? Aren't our births a reflection of cosmic order? After all, couldn't you have been born anywhere? Or, is your birth event as random as the big bang suggests?

You were born on the cusp of your belonging. But your intention to connect to your story makes it real. There is no better place to start connecting to humanity than by looking at the circumstances of your beginning. Reconstruct your identity by seeing your life as one long imperfect story. You can choose your higher self from a crowd of possibilities. Ask yourself why you were born to your particular family? Breathe into that memory, and see what comes to mind.

MY ORIGIN STORY

If Dad had been able to move to the Washington, DC, area when my parents were first married, he would have become a different type of person. But Ma refused to leave her siblings and birthplace. Dad made the most of what life had to offer. He committed to living his life to the fullest. Dad loved to work, and he taught me that when I do not like what I am feeling, I should keep moving until I am too exhausted to worry about it.

Dad's greatest regrets come from the fact that he had to become the head of his household at 13. He felt like he missed a full experience of life when freedom was most accessible to him. While he found many ways to experience fun and enjoyment, especially with his kids, he probably felt he never quite fully pulled it off.

Ma's public life centered around her church. She was serious about applying spiritual principles to everything she said and did. She pretty much demanded the same from her kids as well. We could try to sleep in on Sundays, but until about the age of 16, if you were in her house, you were going to church on Sunday, regardless of where you were the night before. And she meant that.

Ma was committed to being in church and doing her best to follow the laws in the Bible as best as she understood them. Her parents were gracious with all they had. I still hear stories about the times individuals in the community and family found their way to their house just in time to eat. And regardless of who they were, they were always taken care of.

My mother believed in sacrifice and spending her time serving others. "Denying yourself" is what the scriptures command. Like my dad, Ma became the "mother" of her household as a teenager, and regretted the youth and freedom she felt she had lost.

UNDER THE INFLUENCE

You have heard me talk about how close Ma and I were, but I also acknowledge how much I was like my dad. Whenever I felt the need to confront my dad about something she reported to me, he always reminded me of their supposed pact to "keep the kids out of it."

Though they both wanted my allegiance, Dad did not campaign for it. Ma was never so impressed with accolades or honors. She taught me that as long as I was living in a way designed to help someone, I was good with her.

If it ain't helping nobody else, what good is it anyway?

I still love her for that. Most of what I would have changed about my relationship with Ma is my vulnerability. I think I would hide less. I would allow myself to be more known and vulnerable to being hurt.

Ma was more clever with her approach to life in general. If she wanted something, she would get you to suggest it, and then she would agree. Ultimately, she was more interested in staying connected to her siblings, as her father had instilled in her. She is still quietly serving with them in the church community around her.

DISCERNING MY PATH

I know now that I am not just merely the physical creation of my mom and dad. My siblings and I are also their spiritual creations. I was born to those two people, and their negotiations of life had an indelible effect on my identity. That must have been why I was born to them and not someone else.

To discover my authentic self, I have to start with my origin. Then, take my view on what they represent and modulate it higher. My path then becomes about synthesizing the truth in their lives.

My next phase will require that I combine both approaches. Belonging in my authentic life will be about creating a selfless and forward-moving life, picking up at the place where my parents were not able to agree. This is the challenge left to me. This is my evolutionary question, my journey for this lifetime.

THE LIGHT OF CONSCIOUSNESS

No matter what you were told in your childhood, yours is a life without limitations. You were created to be free with agency and power. You are an embodiment of the light of consciousness.

In this play of creation, you have all the energy of unrestrained joy within you, for you have been created in the image of the divine. This divinity will be revealed whenever you choose to experience it.

You are merely part of the divinity in all of the Universe. You were created by desire, will, and urge. You have the same powers that exist in divinity – namely, consciousness, bliss, and freedom. You can choose to experience auxiliary powers caused by the original three. They are the power to will, the power to know, and the power to act.

You can choose a life that is authentic to you. You can find a positive intention that is grounded, sincere, and honest. This joyful self-expression can flow from the core of your being. And this joy will empower you with the capacity to understand what you now only ponder.

THE WISE TEACHER

You will have the intuition of a wise teacher. You will share with the young how the energy flows from your core. Your life will be richer because instead of masking your true self, your essence will be enlightened by the divinity within your soul.

Once you have experienced this greater way of living, the creation assigned to you can achieve its desired end. Then, you will be free to ponder the original questions that started this quest in the first place. For instance, *if everything on the earth is nothing but the expression of divine light, why is life so hard?*

These kinds of questions used to weigh me down. I would be paralyzed with confusion for days and days on end. But now that I am in this place of transformation, I know that there is not a muscle in the body that strengthens itself without resistance. That is in our design.

Can you imagine how tired of people we would be if we were all carbon copies of each other? I enjoy this aspect of diversity. Those who want to become models can do that. And the rest of us can look like we look, and no one gets mad.

THE CHOICE TO BE REBORN IS YOURS

You can choose the path of your mother, father, or both. But maybe you never thought you had a choice.

You are in charge of your fate and your destiny. Both of your parents gave value to your way of life. But both also had aspects that did not work for them. So your authentic life may include aspects of both views. The question for you to play with now is how that becomes real for you.

Honestly, I do not regret the hard choices in my never-ending travels and journeys. I have experienced the tremendous joy and deep pain. Without them, I do not think I could have survived. It makes me see that there is a tomorrow. I need both extremes to realize that life is such a fragile but wonderful thing.

Would be lying if I did not admit that sometimes, I dream of an easier life. But there are costs in trading what you have for what someone else owns. There is a personal cost in that career exchange, lifestyle exchange, and cultural exchange, and there is very little accounting of it, at least there was back then.

So I think I need to acknowledge and own that and not tiptoe around it. It is an important backdrop to what is happening now. I am coming back around. Having gone to all those places I have been and having lived all those lives, I prefer my own story to anyone else's. That is critical. Now, if my dad could hear me say that, he would blow his stack. *What do you have that I didn't give you?* But if he had the courage to own it, he would acknowledge that his value in integrating could have caused us harm. He could honestly say he always tried to do his best for us. And, by and large, he did.

You have spent so much time worrying about the state of the world. You have agonized why the good seem to die young. Yet, none of that energy has changed anything around you. And the world keeps on spinning in the hands of those who play with lives like toys.

But in these last days, you can begin to embrace another story. In different circumstances, your good one day later becomes your evil. There are no absolutes within humanity. Most of these choices are attempts at happiness and freedom from different perspectives. We are all trying to live the best life we can, each from our perspective.

Those who tell the stories rule society.

Plato

I believe that through great trial and tribulation they will come to realize that their destiny is tied up with ours, and their liberation is inextricably and eternally linked to the liberation of all historically oppressed people.

Rev. Dr. Martin Luther King, Jr.

We've all been duped into hating the very people we are created to love.

Unknown

AFIRMATIONS

I am worthy of all the love and grace I receive.

I am rich in emotional, spiritual, and physical health.

I am aware of the energy I bring and the healing I need.

I am generous in extending compassion and empathy to every human being I encounter.

I am healing from the triggers and trauma throughout my ancestors' histories.

CHAPTER FIVE
PLAYING

Bamboo can barely be seen for the first five years as it builds extensive root systems underground before exploding ninety feet into the air within six weeks.

James Clear

In Chapter Four, I outlined my journey to belong. I shared the resistance to change and the defense mechanisms that activate when you move beyond your comfort zone. I described the choice available to become a higher version of yourself when others go low. Finally, I describe the process of reshaping your identity in light of your parents' wins and losses.

Using my life as a guide, you can choose a similar process. When you decide you want to change, you will have to leave the life you have known heretofore. Do not be afraid to critique the familiar when it stands in the way of your new plans. Don't expect your circle to be excited about the changes you make. Prepare to replace your ego-driven instincts with your newly-attuned intuition.

In this final chapter, I will describe the developmental stage of playing. Here I will describe the counter-intuitive benefits of standing still. I will share the calm found on the waves of a crashing ocean. I will conclude by recommending that you rewrite the personal stories from your past that no longer serve your interests.

THE ILLUSION OF CERTAINTY

My childhood paradigm reflected my history of rule-based living. No layperson was an expert in matters of faith or conscience. This was the sole province of the elder.

Through their virtuous lives, they demonstrated an interpretation of the scriptures we all were supposed to follow. They could tell you every step of the way whether you were in accordance with goodwill for your life. If you followed their instructions, you were assured that a rewarding afterlife would follow. On the other hand, if you failed to heed the course they prescribed, there was ex-communication and certain damnation.

This was the center of my identity before my transformation. Of course, there were aspects of this life that were difficult to master. But one thing I had under this paradigm was the illusion of certainty.

I could predict my outcome as long as I followed the rules. The problem with this paradigm is that nothing is certain. It is unpopular to say, but no other words more accurately describe our journey in this universe.

"Man has lost his place at the center of the universe," Dad believed. And like him, I wanted to become a minister and engineer with authority in every field. Like him, I earned my role as a worthy leader and felt assured that no one held any power over me. Now, I no longer chase success. I have learned to be still and accept what I do not know. On this side of my transformation, I am evolving into my authentic self.

Now, I trust my guide, my intuition, and my experience to tell me whether the day was well spent or not.

I have rid my life of the folly of my pious pursuit. It is not an exact science, but it feels so much better than the life I had. Now that the anxiety is gone, I sleep like a baby.

THE STRUGGLE TO ACCEPT YOURSELF

I am learning to appreciate the struggle of life and the freedom that uncertainty provides. It is making me better while keeping me humble. But the alignment I experienced last year does not travel into this one. It is an on-going, energetic process.

The work that I have begun for myself is never done. I have to reaffirm my commitment daily. But I no longer have to check off achievements to feel successful. What I love about my process is the joy I have to share just by being myself.

Before, I had to psyche myself up every day to feel worthy of life. That was under my old paradigm and before I found myself in the hospital. I thought that if I hyed myself up regularly, I could crush it daily.

But in the face of significant loss, the hype game was a non-starter. By staying busy, I ran myself into the ground. I lost all my joy and nearly worked myself to death.

Now, I have learned that the space between my pace and my limits is my breathing room. And regardless of how "successful" I feel, I have more than my vocational work to do. I have to stop. I have to rest. I have to breathe.

When I built my life without breathing room, I poisoned my well. I deprived myself of all my soul was crying out for. I created three treacherous pitfalls I often fell into.

First, my stress levels went through the roof. I did not even realize it, but I could not have a deep conversation with anybody without soon losing my cool. Second, I lost my focus. Things that used to be simple for me to concentrate on, all of a sudden, evaded my grasp. Third, all of my relationships began to suffer. I was either quiet or angry, never in the middle.

What prevented me back then from building breathing room into my lifestyle? In a word, it was fear. First, I had a fear of missing out.

Second, I had a fear of falling behind. Didn't someone say that the early bird gets the worm? All of my friends on social media crush it 24/7, and some weeks it looks like 25/8!

Third, I had a fear of unworthiness. I was never going to gain the attention and love I so desperately needed by just needing it. I had to distinguish myself with my activity and accolades. Right?

BEING MORE BY DOING LESS

But what I realized almost too late is that my fear of being unworthy of love was my biggest distraction. Just when I thought I was doing well, this fear drew me away from what mattered most. Now, I have accepted the fact that I need breathing room. Not just a couple of weeks out of a year which I have irresponsibly referred to as my "vacation." I need regular institutional interventions at the personal level. It is non-negotiable now for me.

What do we glean from creating breathing room in our everyday lives? If we do not work ourselves tirelessly, our work will be multiplied.

By doing less, we will accomplish more. Bet you never thought of the sabbath like that before. Why not?

Our culture thrives on myths of overwork and self-reliance. We have several multi-billion dollar industries based on the promise of wealth. We earn our inheritance if we work ourselves into early graves. For me, it is just not worth it. Sorry, not sorry, but I am done. Find yourself another rat!

Now, if I am ever tempted to skip breathing, I am reminded that the Universe has made promises to those of us who can hear. Don't worry about what you should eat, what you should drink, or what you should wear. I know better than you do. And I have you covered. Literally.

We need to bring our focus back to our breath and allow the universe to fulfill its promise to us. When we prioritize ourselves instead of the work we do for others, our rest will restore the body and the mind.

Since I accepted this journey, I have been resting better than ever. I feel my body returning to a condition of health I have not experienced since high school. All those days and nights of headaches and stress are a thing of the past. My renewal happens not just in sinews and synapses but at the quantum level.

I am so excited to know that you heroes have made it to this chapter on Playing. I have wanted to write this chapter and share it with you for several years now. But it would not have been honest for me to do so at that time.

Sometimes, you get an epiphany about the better version of

yourself that is coming in the future before it manifests. Well, that is what happened to me. I knew this part of the story was coming true for me. But it was only an abstract concept at the time. Now, it is a practice.

I knew I would be playing instead of working into my destiny. But I had to experience that life before I could declare it with authority. Now that time has come. Thank you for being here. Now, let us orient ourselves to our authentic futures together.

ORIENTATION MANUAL TO THE UNIVERSE

We do not get an owner's manual at birth to help us navigate our lives. Instead, we struggle to make sense of all that happens inside and outside of us. Much of the direction we require is written in our stories, myths, and legends. We heard them in pre-school, particularly when it was time for bed.

At bedtime, the mind slows, and our bodies come to lie still. We are tired from our self-inflicted exhaustion from the business of the day. Bedtime is the right time to hear and receive direction from our gracious elders. These fantastic tales of adventure create fantasies in our heads.

As children, we have not been exposed to much of the universe. But we slept with more optimism than our parents had at that age. We grow as stories of the known and unknown conspire to heighten our great awareness. And our potential to be our highest selves grows just the same.

The structure and symbols in dreams stabilize our anxieties. The fears and insecurities color our thoughts and concerns. Grounded with collective wisdom, our understanding can blossom into inspiration. Then, we are ready to choose and own our possibilities. This early process was straightforward when life was simple. But soon, all of our lives became so much more complex. We became better acquainted with anxiety and grief. We did not realize that the stories from our childhood challenge us to master the hero's tests.

UPGRADING OUR THINKING

That is the value of learning how to upgrade your thinking. There is too much at stake now to live a life unprepared. One day, all of life can seem so predictable. But in an instant, chaos can knock you from happy to scared. Now, even when the world grows chaotic, my mind and body remain aligned. In my soul, every day, I am not just grateful; I am excited. And I know that whatever happens, I am made for this.

If the world had been as simple as I thought it was, there would be no need for books like this one. If all I had to do was be prepared as my father suggested, I would have cruised past surviving into thriving. But instead of relying on superstitions and magical thinking spurred by blind faith, I now challenge the lessons from my childhood with the lived experiences of my adult life.

What, then, would I do with my dreams, my surprises, success, and failures? How would I reconcile all the lessons from my parents and my church? How would I embrace the nondual, nonbinary experiences I learned about the universe and humanity with these ancient stories? I had to balance what I was taught with what I experienced. And any of my childhood lessons that no longer worked in my adult life, I discarded.

PRIORITY OF SELF-CARE

When the orientation of my life was mostly economic and practical, eventually, the weights and pressures caused me to lose faith in the universe. I forgot my intention and ended up on my deathbed. I came within a few priceless moments of losing my mortal life on earth.

Looking at it from the outside would have seemed like I was bossing up or leveling up. I was famously demonstrating to friends on social media what success looks like. But I was mostly performing a show or a cover, largely motivated by the fear of becoming irrelevant or being left behind.

The trauma of losing everything seemed like the worst thing that could have happened to me. But experiencing loss helped me decide that I needed to change my paradigm. I responded by developing a healthier life for myself and my family.

EMBRACING OUR CONTEXT

I could not conceive of my hero's journey until I got back to Alabama. I found my writing voice when I found myself back in the land of my ancestors. Here, I would be remiss if I did not note the historical significance of the environment in hero tales of bravery and courage.

The sacredness of the local landscape has always been a fundamental aspect of mythology. Even with the indigenous cultures, who and where you are are related in the cosmic order. We are shaped by their environment and informed by their landscape. These elements are sacred parts of our world and relevant to our journeys.

In Huntsville, Alabama, most people are either in the city or in the suburbs. But if you are in the country, you are connected to current events by Google Fiber. There are very few distractions, so connecting with your higher self is easier. When you are in the country, you sleep underneath a starry sky. You feel connected to your ancestors and something else that is ancient. The archetypal legacy of integrated survival is still breathing and very much alive.

THE COURAGE OF CONNECTION

My dad was a country boy who made good with his options. He maintained his relationship with the land long after his sharecropping days were done. He continued to commune with the ancestors by planting pine trees around his church; there were sacred groves everywhere.

I used to love to walk with Dad through the cemetery on the church grounds. He would reminisce with us about those that had gone before. He knew his offspring could dialogue with them long after he was gone. When I am there, I tell the pines, "I know the man who put you in the ground."

Everything around my parents was alive and breathing. My parents were there because of their livelihood. But they were made richer for their time connected to the land.

Our land connection is a fundamental aspect of humanity. But most of us are isolated, living on the islands we create. We are bound by our fear of what we do not know. Instead of groves of pine trees, we are encompassed by virtual worlds or brick, rock, and stone.

Our land is enriched with hidden, magical potentialities. The choice of connection remains the same. Though I do not have the burden of caring for the land, I choose to connect with it because I am a part of the same nature.

LIVING IN A SACRED WAY

In this new paradigm and practice in which I find myself, I have developed an ability to build a sacred place out of the mundane. Our nature is to hide behind walls in this age of chaos. Even in the middle of the pandemic and the age of social distance, I had to find pathways in nature.

Contrary to the walls that protected me as a kid, these paths elevated me from my psyche and other human limitations. I would find a bench in Panera next to the fireplace. I disconnected myself from Facebook notifications and all other cares of this distracted world. Then, I waited for the words you find on this page.

I do not owe anybody that time, energy, or creativity. In this place, I put in my earbuds and feel what my soul is becoming. I turn on an intentional frequency of sound and simply feel the flow.

This is my place of creative incubation. In those hidden hours, I ignore whatever happens outside myself. This is where I dream, write, and connect with my divinity.

When I first found this space, I noticed that often nothing happens. I could not stay here for very long at first. I would leave and go to Applebees with no expectation of returning. I was embarrassed that I had distracted myself again.

But by consistently creating my sacred space, something eventually happened. The energy that I needed to prepare this space manifested. With no invocation, this guidance came and found me.

I had created, by ritual, an emotional space within my body. I imagined being in the presence of future friends and colleagues. That is when consciousness woke me up from my spiritual slumber and I traveled to the moment we are sharing now.

How does this sacred place compare to the place where myths and legends are made? How does the 21st-century communal space compare to the primitive place the indigenous hunter found on the plains? It is the same.

Mama Anna tried to show me how to connect to our ancestors. In indigenous cultures, the entire world is a sacred place. Now, I no longer have to pretend to enjoy the unnatural. My authentic life is a much better trip. And what is even better, it is all mine.

THE FOLLY OF A PURPOSE-DRIVEN LIFE

The spiritual practice of my childhood was very much about life's destination. According to my childhood stories, everything in life has a reason for being. Even the universe needs purpose to exist. Some of us then called it a "grand vision" or a "master plan."

One day we'll wake up, and it will just all be better. The world is a complete mess but don't worry, just be happy.

I cannot tell you how many gospel songs were based on this pie-in-the-sky theology. Even though some of them provided fond memories, the songs were dangerous for me.

The idea that we have to wait to die to be happy is simply

for the birds. This teaching helps many "influencers" gain legions of followers. But those followers never expected to experience fulfillment during their lives on earth. Maybe that is what makes these ideas so appealing.

You cannot have a revolutionary attitude with colonial practices. When you did not know any better, you were not expected to improve. But now that consciousness has found you, you are accountable for your lack of imagination. And it is not just your life's happiness that gets delayed; it affects generations to come.

THE EVER-PRESENT JOY OF BEING

Actually, we are already in the fullness of perfect peace. We do not have to wait until we die for it to happen. There is no future moment when happiness will be more possible than it is right now. But we cannot be lazy in the meantime.

This teaching is called the doctrine of divine play. From this perspective, the Universe is said to be in divine play, but not in the sense that every day is fun. Play, in this sense, is anything that is done purely for its own sake. We are not to live for a result to be experienced after our deaths. Now, in any and every experience, I can choose to experience joy.

Here, of course, joy is not ecstatic happiness. It is not a feeling or performance of positivity. This joy is like an easy Sunday morning.

This type of joy comes from accepting all that is loving and gracious in every moment. We have, within our bodies, the capacity to benefit from whatever is happening in any situation. We can tap into the whole of any experience with a loving acceptance of all that is. I have found that by committing myself to my process of growth and ever-expanding consciousness, fullness and joy come as soon as I make room for them. In this way of living, all of my delays and failures along the way will only sweeten my eventual arrival into my higher existence. Now that I have tasted the fruit, I will always find my way back to it.

THE TOIL OF INNER WORK

Do not get me wrong. I am not saying that my new lifestyle is easygoing. I still have daily work I have to do. It is just that in my work, I do not have to prove anything to myself or anyone else. This work is internal and requires a daily deposit into my lifestyle.

Inner work becomes a lifestyle the same way as eating healthy or working out. I experience the depth of the life I build. My progress is incremental and contagious.

Every once in a while, I wake up elevated from one level to the next. But what I experience consistently now is a gentle leading guide. Then, suddenly, something that had been hiding for several days will all at once be there.

I find I am moving into an ever-growing acceptance of myself. This energy creates in me reverence also for those around me. And now, with every breath, I have become more connected without condition.

THE WOUNDED HEALER

Even though my feelings still get hurt occasionally, my real nature, my authentic self, is never wounded. I have a balm I apply to my open heart that allows me to heal from scars that never go past the surface. It is like those movies where the hero is shot in the chest wearing a bulletproof vest.

Now, I level up and start that round again. But, I come back with more heart than I ever had before. I am ever vigilant in protecting those around me. I have the kind of courage that befits a champion fighter. I resembled a winner under my perfectionist persona. But my true hero core was shaped in this new paradigm.

I want you to uncover your truth and find rest in that place. If you are like me, that place will not be where you have been praised or celebrated the most. You may be the only one in your life who knows anything about it.

THE INSPIRATION OF HERO STORIES

I have always loved reading sacred texts like the Quran or the Bible. Reading epic hero stories creates in me a sense of awe. Isn't that the whole point of reading anything?

None of us has to go far off the interpreted path to find ourselves in very difficult situations. I can honestly say that where I thought I would lose, I gained. The courage to face the trials and to bring into ourselves a whole new range of real possibilities for others to experience — that is the hero's deed.

I have also found much courage in my dreams to find new myths and stories. Whatever it is that my ego does not want me to acknowledge or deal with — that is what I dream about.

THE PRIVATE AWAKENING OF YOUR HERO

I have been here for a couple of years, having a pure and direct experience of grace and love. This awakening is slowly grounding my actions and my very being. It allows me to be still when, in years past, I could only move in an attempt to distract myself from what I did not like about my life.

Because of the culture in which I live, I do not have many people that I can talk to about this awakening, so I keep it mostly to myself. But I have decided to publish it in anticipation of the day when our soul care becomes something we can talk about with our closest friends and family. I hope and pray that day is already here.

I experience love as something much more than personal but rather unlimited in all dimensions and aspects that we can perceive. I now prefer to think of this love as merely a consciousness. It permeates my entire being on every level and is perceptible by all.

THE JOY OF BEING YOUR INTEGRATED SELF

I am certain we are the embodiment of this love. This free and independent source of redemptive energy is available to all. I believe this love and consciousness hides most of its nature from creation. But we can experience it on whatever level we are mature enough to handle.

You may one day wake up feeling overwhelmed. The memory of all of the times before when you were not true to yourself can make you sick to your stomach. No matter how good you become at realizing your divinity, all of the knee-jerk reactions of your past will still be there.

In the process of pretending, you put your own life at risk. This memory might trigger you as it does me. That is the normal reaction in the human experience.

But that will not always be the way you respond. It is like moving to a new state after having spent years in the same old place. Your memories travel with you, but they will not always throw you into chaos.

Learn to accept your journey and be patient with yourself. You spent decades being fragile. You will not become secure overnight. Even with access to a healthy, divine core, the energy within you must flow naturally. This flow will bless you and those around you. But, until you accept it, complete freedom is still a hope for you.

Then, once you embrace all your history, you will be as free as the birds. You will be motivated to maintain a practice that supports an understanding of your completion process. As you learn to master it, you will begin to be excited about it and share it with those you love.

As you begin to know yourself completely and apologetically, may your light of awareness shine in every shadow where your misunderstandings still confuse and confound. May you become a perfect example of divine grace in this world until you are ready to pass these lessons on to someone else.

Well, sometimes you need to destroy somethin' to save it. That is in the Bible. Or the Constitution.
Jason Stackhouse

Please don't try to understand others, that is not the way. Try to understand yourself. You are a miniature Universe. In you, the whole map of existence.

Osho

AFFIRMATIONS

I am the image of God in the universe.

I am endowed with the power to control my responses to emotional triggers.

I am valuable to humanity not because of my achievement but by sheer virtue of my being.

I am capable of experiencing joy in the most difficult set of circumstances.

I am authorized to create a sacred space everywhere I go.

I am committed to representing my authentic self in my well-being for all creation to witness.

MEET THE AUTHOR

Chauncey is the son of LaVerta Moore and Dave McGlathery, the former pastor of Pine Grove Missionary Baptist Church and a pioneer in the civil rights movement. His father launched Chauncey on a path towards the destruction of all barriers to wealth and wellness. Chauncey is a public health social justice advocate and policy and advocacy manager for community-based health organizations in the U.S.. He trained at Auburn University School of Engineering, earning a Bachelor of Science Degree in Electrical Engineering, Howard University School of Law, earning a Doctor of Jurisprudence and Beeson Divinity School, earning a Masters of Divinity.

Chauncey was admitted to the federal bar of the Southern and Eastern Districts of New York and practiced law with some of the most well known civil rights attorneys in the country. He was a member of the Special Federal Litigation division and specialized in Section 1983 of Title 42, which allows federal review of alleged state civil rights violations. While in New York, Chauncey defended the City of New York and its Police and Correction Departments in civil rights cases under the Giuliani administration. While in Boston, Chauncey received additional leadership training from many institutions including Harvard University, Tufts University and the Interaction Institute. Most recently he served as an adjunct professor in the African and African Diaspora Studies Department at Boston College. Chauncey selects a few individuals to privately coach along the path of the hero's journey. Connection to that work can be found on his website: www.chaunceysvirtualcoaching.com. Chauncey is regularly invited to present The Hero's Journey at global conferences relating to health, wellness, and society.

Scan this QR code using your smartphone's camera for more information about the author.

STAY CONNECTED

Thank you for reading, *Choose Your Own Adventure: An Orientation Manual to the Universe*. Chauncey looks forward to connecting with you. Here are a few ways you can connect with the author and stay updated on new releases, speaking engagements, products, and more.

FACEBOOK	Chauncey of The MindfulFamily
INSTAGRAM	@chaunceymcglathery_
WEBSITE	www.chaunceysvirtualcoaching.com
EMAIL	cm@chaunceymcglathery.com

www.ingramcontent.com/pod-product-compliance
Lightning Source LLC
Chambersburg PA
CBHW020307010526
44107CB00001B/17